Frederick Valentich

Double Dark

Cape Otway, Victoria, Australia

Frederick Valentich

Double Dark

A True Story

Victor F. Bongiorno

First published by Busybird Publishing 2025

Copyright © 2025 Victor F. Bongiorno

ISBN:
Paperback: 978-1-923501-47-8
Ebook: 978-1-923501-48-5

Victor F. Bongiorno has asserted his right under the Copyright, Designs and Patents Act 1988 to be identified as the author of this work. The information in this book is based on the author's experiences and opinions. The publisher specifically disclaims responsibility for any adverse consequences, which may result from the use of the information contained herein. Permission to use information has been sought by the author. Any breaches will be rectified in further editions of the book.

All rights reserved. No part of this publication may be reproduced, stored in or introduced into a retrieval system, or transmitted in any form, or by any means (electronic, mechanical, photocopying, recording or otherwise) without the prior written permission of the author. Any person who does any unauthorised act in relation to this publication may be liable to criminal prosecution and civil claims for damages. Enquiries should be made through the publisher.

Cover image: Kev Howlett, Busybird Publishing

Cover design: Busybird Publishing

Layout and typesetting: Busybird Publishing

Editor: Busybird Publishing

Busybird Publishing
2/118 Para Road
Montmorency, Victoria
Australia 3094
www.busybird.com.au

In Memoriam
Tom Butler

"Three things that cannot be long hidden: the sun, the moon, and the truth"

~Buddha.

Fred's Plaque, Cape Otway, Victoria.

Foreword

"... I've got the bullets. Who's got the bazooka?"
Paul Keating

A recent life-changing event in the form of a complicated heart operation in April 2023 has given me the purpose to tell the story of missing aviator Frederick Valentich, which occurred late one evening off the coast of southern Australia in October 1978.

Setting out all the credible evidence will allow others to make their own critical assessment of that event, evidence that has never properly come to light because of what was by all accounts a flawed investigation by the relevant authorities.

What surprised me as I collated and navigated the jigsaw puzzle of information leading to a conclusion was that along the way, I had also found myself drawn to young Frederick, the person he was and the difficulties he had encountered as he set about achieving his career goal of becoming an airline pilot.

It became obvious to me that I have had a parallel life with him, and so I am sympathetic to the personal challenges he had faced as a young, underfunded, and enthusiastic career pilot from an Italian immigrant family living in Avondale Heights, Melbourne, in 1970s Australia.

In those days, such lofty ambitions of becoming an airline pilot were unusual, and it could be said that Fred was shooting for the stars, which he was, but it also says a lot about the quality of the person.

What started as a recorded interview with a retired King Island beef farmer using an old Walkman cassette player back in 2001 has not only developed into a critical analysis of Fred's last minutes but also a synopsis of my own life as well.

As I let the story develop in my head, what is apparent is that not only am I unable to disassociate the two, but that I am comfortable with the outcome, and so, as a natural progression, there is a lot of my own life in this book as well.

This book is not a running dialogue of immutable facts. It is a story and a mystery, and as such, colourful references are sometimes used to make a point, but never has there been any compromise in relating the hard facts regarding the disappearance of lone pilot Frederick Valentich.

One of my biggest qualifications in writing this book is that I am not a UFO watcher. I do not belong to any registered UFO organisation, and other than while researching this matter, I generally take little interest in UFOs.

However, after having investigated the facts of this and other related cases, I now do believe in the existence of UFOs and I am also open to the possibility that they are of non-human intelligence (NHI).

It is also incumbent on all reading this to "open their mind" as to what may have occurred one clear evening over Bass Strait, Victoria, Australia.

I am in no doubt that Fred, in the aviation parlance, "had company" that evening but nothing can be determined in this work as to what the craft was or where it came from.

For me, the fact that he was not alone is not in dispute, and that he was also the victim of fate by simply being in the wrong place at the wrong time and that the decisions he made in the dying minutes of daylight that day precipitated the creation of this enduring aviation mystery.

At that time, NASA had already pre-empted making contact with extraterrestrial life, placarding and broadcasting relevant statistical information from satellites Voyager 1 (launched 5th of September 1977) and Voyager 2 (launched 20th of August 1977, prior to

Voyager 1) which give the specific details of Earth's location in the galaxy as they plunge ever deeper into interstellar space.

Not only is this evidence that the agency is keeping an open mind to the chance of intelligent life existing in the never-ending outer limits of space, but also that this intelligent life form is friendly.

No doubt this altruistic liberal approach could have been an advantage when seeking congressional backing on the day, but in this case, the pursuit of science is no mandate for being so supremely naïve and reckless with our interstellar security.

If there's a chance of encountering intelligent life at all, the risks are a complete unknown.

The launch of both craft pre-dated Fred's encounter by over 12 months, but that is only an observation and nothing further is inferred or implied in the making of that statement.

I would also like to preface this work by saying that UAP, is an acronym which originally stood for "Unidentified 'Aerial' Phenomena", later amended to the broader definition of "Unidentified 'Anomalous' Phenomena".

As a child of the 1950s, it would be fair to say that I am of an older generation. To me, the use of the term UAP is a somewhat woke attempt to appear authoritative, endeavouring to add something cerebral and profound to the narrative, when in fact, it adds nothing at all.

It complicates the uncomplicated.

I generally choose to use the simple acronym UFO, which has a certain unmitigated honesty and earthiness about itself, and at the end of the day, it's just a lot easier to say.

My undertaking is to write this book based on the accumulated knowledge and testimonies, gained over a 25-year period while I owned and operated a small air charter business at Apollo Bay on Victoria's rugged south coast.

Apollo Bay is 7 nautical miles or 13 kilometres from Cape Otway, where Frederick Valentich had made his last position report to

Melbourne Flight Service, and so this mystery justifiably belongs to Apollo Bay.

With the information that has been gathered over that period, I am committed to conveying the facts and events as clearly and truthfully as I can, while I still can.

As they must, some chapters concentrate on the more technical aspects of the investigation to make this work as definitive and comprehensive as possible.

Keep the faith and push through those chapters to what I think is a long-awaited explanation that has been hiding in plain sight for almost five decades.

This journey for me has been both compelling and revealing, not all pertaining to Fred's disappearance but also of something else: the unwillingness of the investigators to both tell all they know or to uncover all that there was to know.

It will also be observed that my mindset with respect to those authorities altered throughout my investigation as the truth became apparent.

Finally, let me thank my many contributors and my two dogs, Rosie and George, who provided the unconditional support that was so essential to the completion of this project, every day sleeping patiently and faithfully beside or under my desk.

Every day until 5 pm, that is.

To date, the disappearance of Frederick Valentich has been one of the world's most enduring unsolved aviation mysteries, and the weight of evidence suggests to me that something extraordinary occurred just off Cape Otway, Victoria, Australia, on the evening of the 21st of October 1978.

Contents

Foreword	1
1 - Dark days	7
2 - The credibility gap	13
3 - The preceding years	16
4 - Apollo Bay	18
5 - Close encounters	21
6 - I see the man	30
7 - An inquiry gone wrong	33
8 - Headwinds	50
9 - The flight plan and the flight	55
10 - Spatial disorientation	67
11 - Pending legal action	73
12 - Restricted airspace penetration	75
13 - A handwritten letter	82
14 - The Cape Otway Lighthouse log	91
15 - The DoT Accident & Incident Report	95
16 - Ross	100
17 - Rhonda Rushton	107
18 - The engagement ring and plans for the future	114
19 - Steve Robey	119
20 - Merv O'Meara	121
21 - The elephant in the room	137
22 - John	142
23 - Mick	147

24 - Roy Manifold	149
25 - Edith	151
26 - Air Vice-Marshal Alan Reed	154
27 - The Coroner's Report	156
28 - Brian	159
29 - Just one more thing	165
30 - The ATSB and NASA	168
31 - The power of circumstantial evidence	173
32 - The final minutes	175
33 - The last word	196
34 - Per ardua ad astra	202
About the Author	205

1

Dark days

"… still a man hears what he wants to hear and disregards the rest."
Paul Simon

"Police, Fire or Ambulance?" to which I replied "Ambulance" almost hoping that would be the last of the questions.

It was an illogical hope that nothing else, no more questions and no more answers, would be required. I had taken the giant step. I had acknowledged that I was not at all well by calling you. *Isn't that enough? Now, let's please just get it over with.*

In recognition of the impact this singular action was going to have on my life, my whole person was suddenly regretting making the call.

Maybe I would like to just forget this whole thing? Maybe if I just hung up, the pain would be gone and I could just go back to sleep?

But maybe not.

My dogs, sensing something irregular, stood staring in the darkness … watching mute.

Then the fateful question followed, the one I'd been dreading, and it was inevitable. "Why do you need the ambulance?"

I went cold. Colder than I already was.

I hesitated for a split second, but I was committed, committed to ending my aviation career and sending my whole professional and personal life into a tailspin.

Sitting erect in the darkness and aloneness of my bedroom, both fists clamped over my chest region … as if compression would help and summoning the last of my dignity, I replied, "Chest pain."

They were the very last words I would ever utter as Chief Pilot.

What began in Nairobi in 1979 at the end of an overland trip when, as a young man, I had pawned my coveted Olympus OM-1 camera and lenses to take my first flying lessons out over the sprawling plains of East Africa, had ended so unceremoniously at 3 am in a dark bedroom with three retrievers to bear witness.

I was a commercial pilot and, worse than that, I was a rare breed. I was a self-employed commercial pilot and as company chief pilot without a current medical, the whole operation was effectively grounded, forthwith.

I had cooked my professional goose and in that instant, all the doors in my career had slammed shut. Given my age of 68 years and the complicated bureaucratic processes required to redress the situation, they would never be re-opened.

The work had ended, and I was unemployed.

I was entirely on my own after that, and boy, I felt it.

The hollow feeling in my stomach that followed was almost worse than the chest pain.

For better or for worse, my life had changed forever, and there was no going back.

I can't recall what transpired afterwards or the operator's response. I was along for the ride from that point on, a feeling I would become quite familiar with in the months that followed.

The operator continued with her list of questions. She was good at her job. Thorough and calm. I responded to her instructions with resignation.

She followed procedure and went through her routine. She asked about access to the property and what medication I was on if any, and whether I had any aspirin in the house.

Later in the ambulance, lying on my back, I deliberately watched the streetlights flash past. No sirens, no lights. It was four o'clock in the morning.

I felt every bump in the road. I tried to pick the route and anticipate the turns, but I lost track. I was always so used to being in control, but this was no longer my rodeo. Not anymore.

I had cobbled together a quick text with instructions for the care of my beloved dogs and then I had walked out, without even thinking to take a toothbrush.

More questions on the way. "Victor, do you have private health insurance? Which hospital would you like to attend?" *I get a choice!?* "Do you have any symptoms like a sore throat or runny nose? And can you please just hold still while I jam this stick up your old nose?" Goes with the territory.

That was my first ever COVID test, and now there was no avoiding it. I had always relied on self-healing, the body healing itself type of thing. It had seemed to work in the past.

I was grateful for the care. *What a great country we live in*, I thought to myself.

At the hospital, as I lay on the trolley in the corridor, the ambos waited and chatted. It was a warm and very welcome conversation. I even felt that the young paramedic was about to hold my hand. I would have welcomed it.

They stayed a while longer than they were obliged to stay and I felt guilty about that.

I thanked them, and they left.

I was no longer Chief Pilot. I wasn't even able to fly. I was worried about my dogs, my clients, and my aircraft that were sitting grounded in two states and I felt very much alone.

It was 3 am on the morning of the 19th of November 2022, when I made that call, and I was in cardiac care for six days. I wasn't operated on until the 6th of April 2023, four and a half months later.

It was complicated.

It was mid-December 2023 and I was rifling through the remains of the boxes I had unearthed in the backrooms and cupboards of my little house opposite the Apollo Bay Airfield in Marengo. I had to get out. It was a fire sale; the business was closed and the flying was over, for good.

These were boxes of what was mostly forgotten, unused junk, a treasure trove of memories and not always pleasant ones. They'd sit there for decades and then you clean them and sort them just as you leave, remarking to yourself how great the place finally looks.

It was a thankless job that could no longer be avoided.

After 23 years, I was committed to selling off what I could of the flying operation, and the little house at Marengo needed to be tenanted, sooner rather than later.

I recalled a question long ago from a briefing solicitor about my predicament, whatever it was at the time, I forget. He mused, "I see …" as he doodled on the pad on the desk in front of him. "I see … and is it running you or are you running it?" Funny the things that pop into your head. Well, *it* was definitely running me now. No question.

The surgeons hadn't decided on a plan of attack for my heart operation, and I really shouldn't have been doing anything at all, but sitting idle wasn't an option either. I was struggling to stabilise my mental health and doing nothing wouldn't help.

I decided if it was my time, then so be it. That's God's department.

I chose mental health over physical health, and I elected to stay as active as I could given my circumstances.

No more flying that beautiful coast out past Cape Otway and the Moonlight Head to the Twelve Apostles rock stacks, and in all sorts of weather.

No more Shipwreck Coast, and no more rolling breakers, whales, dolphins, the Great Southern Ocean. No more tall timber of the Otways that I had come to know so well, or the history of all the souls that inhabited that lonely region.

And what surprised me the most. No more people.

I mean that in a nice way.

Without realising it, over the last 25 years, I had become a people person. I had dealt with many and varied travellers from all corners of the globe. I had become addicted to the parry and thrust of selling this product. This wild place.

I'd taken it for granted so many times before. Thousands of times, and now it was over.

Forever.

The Twelve Apostles

Loch Ard Gorge and the Twelve Apostles

Both offices closed, grounded aircraft in two states, no income, no lifestyle, and a heart running on three cylinders.

The whole thing was fucked, really fucked.

They were dark days indeed.

2

The credibility gap

Forlorn and alone, yet to be emptied and standing in the middle of the floor of the little Marengo house, was the old piano stool.

Curious how empty rooms always smell dusty.

Under the seat was a compartment that used to hold piano music. Now, it was full of all sorts of other things, and I dreaded opening it. One just gets so tired of that thankless task of sifting through memories and making hard decisions.

Inside were music books, Peter Allen, Jim Croce and a guidebook, *Walking the Otways*. Pens, tie pins, keys and a small cassette tape wrapped by a rubber band with a note written in blue ballpoint pen that simply read "Victor".

There it lay, the old cassette tape, misplaced and long forgotten. Evidence relating to a mystery.

In the early days, not long after arriving in Apollo Bay, I had been passionate about this. I'd done a lot of research on the disappearance of a young aviator, something that had occurred not that very far from where I was standing.

My enquiries had been initiated by the contents of this cassette, and so too this cassette was a part of the mystery for me.

Finding it again had opened a flood of memories. I remembered the investigation and the interviews. The contemplation and the research.

Now, more than ever and faced with my own mortality, faced with the inevitability of the onset of the twilight of my years and still committed to the memory of a brave young pilot I had grown to respect and admire, I realised that the time had come.

No more delays or the questions raised in this aviation mystery that had once generated so much interest would remain unanswered, and this small corner of Australian aviation history would forever be incomplete.

I know things, I thought to myself. I know things that no one else does, and I felt connected to the long-past and controversial events that had occurred 44 years earlier.

I had a sense of duty bestowed on me to bridge what I saw as the credibility gap, the gap that existed between truth and non-truth, between what I've been told and what I believe actually occurred.

If not me, then who? I had come full circle.

As I reflected and reconstructed the order of the facts over the ensuing months, the story eventually came to be a welcome safe place in my mind … somewhere to retreat to. Somewhere to be positive and creative and to disconnect from the reality of my life … and I clung to it.

Time is short and this is a story that needs to be told truthfully and with respect.

It is a compelling Australian aviation mystery, but it is important to keep an open mind to appreciate it fully.

An open mind is like an open parachute as it catches all the available air and gently lowers its cargo, but if it collapses, then the individual plummets to earth in a terminal spiral and without hope.

This is the story of an event that occurred late one evening off the coast of Cape Otway with a lone pilot departing Melbourne's Moorabbin Airport for what was to be a routine three-hour return night flight to King Island in the Bass Strait.

The lighthouse at Cape Otway, built in 1848, was then the gateway to Australia as it welcomed immigrants in clipper ships to the new world down under.

While historically embodying all the hope of the new world, it would also become a metaphor for tragedy and heartbreak when, during the Australian Gold Rush, sailing ships travelling non-stop from Liverpool, heavy under canvas and with their occupants having endured months of privation on the open sea, would enter Bass Strait from the southwest.

Bound for Hobsons Bay, Melbourne, history records they were often suddenly and unexpectedly smashed to matchwood at journey's end, succumbing to the rocky reefs and headlands on what would later become known as Victoria's "Shipwreck Coast".

I would come to know every reef and every rockface along that coast as part of my workplace, and for years flying it in all sorts of weather was my daily routine.

Over the last two centuries, this cape with its tragic shipwreck history has witnessed many souls in various stages of distress.

On the evening of the 21st of October 1978, it saw yet one more soul alone in distress with the disappearance of 20-year-old pilot Frederick Valentich and his four-seat Cessna 182L aircraft, Australian registration mark VH-DSJ.

Outside of radar coverage and under stress from another craft pursuing him at close quarters, Frederick engaged in a final six-minute radio discussion with Melbourne Flight Service describing the characteristics of his unknown and hitherto unacknowledged pursuer.

To date, nothing has ever been found of Frederick or his aircraft.

3

The preceding years

Prior to moving to Apollo Bay, I had owned a small 500-acre fine wool property in the Western District of Victoria for four years from 1994 to 1998.

To anyone who knows anything about life on the land, 500 acres isn't a "living area" – meaning it's generally accepted that one can't make a living off of it, but I thought I would be the exception.

They were wonderful years, but while living out there, I'd come to learn one of life's inconvenient truths: time and reality are willing bedfellows.

Solitude is a bit like protein; you can't live off it alone, and while lifestyle is optional, an income is mandatory.

The then 5-year tax averaging rule for agriculture had calculated my average taxable annual income was $3,195 per annum, with an actual income of zero for the last three of those years. That, and a budget of sixty dollars a week for both food and fuel hadn't worked.

The good year had never happened. I was worn out.

Ultimately, I sold to neighbouring Nareen Station and left for "where the peoples is", unsure of where that would eventually be.

Driving down along the coast of Western Victoria, I searched for a new place of abode. Peterborough was too expensive and full of retired Western District farmers. A conservative place like I'd known too well, and I needed more this time.

I headed eastwards through the Otways which were beautiful, but again, still a bit too remote. It had probably been 40 years since I'd been there, and I had no recollection of the geography at ground level.

Before the farm, I had worked as a commercial pilot, having obtained and held an airline standard of flying licence (Air Transport Pilot Licence or ATPL) but regrettably, for one reason or another, I had never utilised it.

Spilt milk now, as they say, and if I were to be completely honest, that life was probably going to be a bit too formal for me anyway.

Previously, when the cloud was low and the weather wouldn't allow me to fly direct to Melbourne, I had occasionally tracked coastal via the Shipwreck Coast and the mist-shrouded Otway Hills, while scud running in an aircraft loaded up with crayfish out of Kingston and Millicent in South Australia, unaware of just how familiar I would eventually become with that coastline.

This was in the pre-GPS, pre-digital and pre-connectivity era. Paper maps and charts and flight plans spread across my knees, following pencil lines as best I could while avoiding the worst of the storms and all the time amending my waypoint ETAs to a never-quietened, nosey and demanding Melbourne Flight Service operator who, for all I knew, on occasions may well have been Steve Robey.

Steve Robey was the Melbourne Flight Service duty officer on the other end of the radio for Frederick Valentich's fateful, last flight.

4

Apollo Bay

Driving east, the very next town of any size was Apollo Bay.

When entering the town from the west, Telford Street, the airport street, is one of the first streets encountered at the bottom of the big hill. The sign read "Airport" pointing left, and for me, it was a beacon, especially in those days.

Pilots always like to visit small country airfields in the same way that tourists like to visit cathedrals. It's just what they do.

Often, the tourists visit cathedrals to pay their respects and admire the architecture, and paradoxically, some pilots also visit small airfields for the same reason, to pay their respects.

A holy place for some, where on occasions they too had spoken to God while in the act of taking off or landing.

Over the subsequent years, I had observed them come and go from the privacy of my airport office window. Standing at the airport fence in a contemplative mode, staring into the middle distance, alone with their thoughts, they spoke their silent prayers to their god of the airfield, finishing with a glance skyward before moving on.

And so, predictably, I had turned left that day at the airport, sign in my beaten-up Subaru Brumby utility with two kelpies, Bill and Harley hanging out over the back, all searching for a new life together.

Just fifty metres from the Great Ocean Road, opposite the airport gate, there was a house with a sign in the front yard that read "Scenic Flights. Enquire here" … and right next to it was another sign that read "For Sale".

And so, predictably, I had turned left that day

The decision was made before the wheels of the little car had stopped rolling.

I couldn't believe my luck as I felt the pressure subsiding, all only one hundred meters from the Marengo surf beach.

In the 1980s, I had worked up in Far North Queensland as a commercial pilot spruiking for fare-paying passengers up and down the main street of Cairns, selling flights out over the Great Barrier Reef on up to Cooktown.

I had reason to remind myself of this now.

I had skills, and I had energy.

Lots of it.

It was 1998, and business was challenging but rewarding.

I was 44 years young, and Apollo Bay was a breath of fresh air. People, surf and a chance to make a living doing something I loved:

flying punters around Cape Otway to the Twelve Apostles and out to King Island. It was miles and metaphorical miles from the farm.

I wrote my own script, and the years slipped away.

Apollo Bay. 2016

The Apollo Bay Aviation flight base

5

Close encounters

The recorded interview on a cassette tape that I had found in an old piano stool was the original motivating force that launched me down the path of this investigation to look deeper into the facts surrounding the disappearance of Frederick Valentich. Facts that were now almost becoming Chinese whispers, harder to verify and fading rapidly with the passage of time.

The tape was a record of a mysterious UFO encounter that had occurred on King Island in the late 1970s. More importantly, it was with a person I had known and trusted, and believed to be both credible and of sound mind.

Her name was Vivienne Baldock, and at the time of the interview, she was 81 years of age. I had known the family for many years.

At the time, both her testimony on the tape together with other evidence that I had turned up seemed compelling to me.

Early in the investigation, when the faith had good duco, I couldn't understand why people and the authorities weren't getting on board to support and help me solve this in the face of what I saw as compelling new evidence on one of the world's great aviation mysteries.

The question remained in the back of my mind as to why I had not persisted with the original line of investigation all those years ago. Slowly, as I stood there, it came back to me and I recalled that, at the time, there had been a lot of negative feedback.

Many had advised that I should drop it, and that he "wasn't quite right" mentally, that Fred was less than competent, strange, and a bit of a mystery man.

It was a common thread, and I had let this affect me.

Knowing what I know now about Fred and having the experience as chief pilot of my own air charter company for over 20 years, nothing could be further from the truth.

We often like to think that we have broad shoulders and that we can soldier on regardless of what anyone else thinks, but it wears one down like water dripping on stone and at the end of the day, it inevitably had an effect on me and my self-confidence.

But I found I couldn't quite let it go.

As soon as becoming airborne out of Marengo airfield, I had flown past the controversial location of Fred's disappearance, passing it thousands of times over the years while en route to the Twelve Apostles rock stacks, a popular local tourist destination.

Years ago I had loaned the cassette to a local media personality and while I am unsure what had transpired, at some point he had returned the tape leaving it with one of of my pilots.

It obviously wasn't evening news material, and so it had found its way into the old piano stool, and there it had remained for nearly 20 years.

I couldn't recall if he said he had listened to the recording or not, but when I eventually found a clapped-out old tape player to re-listen to it myself, I wouldn't have blamed him if he hadn't.

The player that I eventually acquired was dusty and squeaked a lot as it turned. Maybe a bit too much, I thought as I loaded it in and pressed "play". I thought that if it chews up my tape, I'll be screwed. Even more screwed than I already was.

Originally recorded in 2001 on a "state-of-the-art" Walkman cassette tape player, I realised that it was of poor quality, and listening to it required focus and commitment.

As the interviewer, I had waffled on a lot in an effort to set the scene for the mysterious event that had occurred on King Island over 25 years before.

At the time, I had asked a few questions to prove that the interviewee was of sound mind, things like family history and dates, even the score for the recent Pat Rafter game at the Australian Open. Vivienne didn't disappoint with prompt and clear responses. Silly really, but that was what I thought to be important at the time, and as it happens, I'm pleased I did.

Vivienne and her late husband, Kevin, had owned a farm on the Loop Road at Lymwood on King Island for many years. It was the family farm and on it they raised six children, living there for 42 years from 1952 to 1994. They then sold the property and retired to Nimbin in northern NSW.

Nimbin had and still has a certain reputation. When I told people that the interviewee lived there, generally the response was, "Oh yeah, man, Nimbin, there would be lots of UFOs up there." Used to make me smile.

They had chosen to swap the more temperate climate of King Island for the tropical environment of the Northern Rivers in New South Wales and to be close to their daughter Lois in their final years.

In 2001, I drove up from Apollo Bay to pay Vivienne a visit, and I had brought with me a Walkman tape player to record her encounter with a UFO that she told me had occurred one dark and cloudy King Island night.

As verified by the family, Kevin was also mostly present at the time of the encounter so this adds a lot of credibility to the sighting. It happened sometime in the late 1970s, but I can't be more specific than that.

On that night, Kevin was readying the car at the rear of the house, and together they were about to drive into the local town of Currie, midway down the west side of the island, to attend a Returned Services League army meeting, for which Kevin was secretary.

Meanwhile, Vivienne had walked out to open the front gate, waiting for Kevin to bring the car around to the front of the house.

They had turned off all the lights in and around the house as they departed, so everything was dark and still.

Vivienne described the bright light that suddenly and without warning fell from the sky at tremendous speed, stopping abruptly and hovering silently just above the front gate.

I can only think that she showed enormous courage in standing her ground in an effort to try and identify the object. Many wouldn't have.

She related that it had no downward beam and it hung there at or just above treetop height in complete silence, and in very close proximity to her.

She thought it may have been an aircraft about to crash to the ground in front of her, lifting her arms in a gesture of defence. But it had abruptly stopped short, hovering silently. She said that it was about as big as the full moon and that it took her breath away.

She emphasised that it was completely without sound and that it had eventually turned a blueish colour, which is consistent with other publicised reported paranormal sightings I had read about, both here and in America.

Her recall was consistent and precise as she spoke of the close encounter with the UFO, hovering and moving on various occasions at great speed around her local area, before abruptly coming to a dead stop.

These flight characteristics are consistent with other UFO sightings and with Frederick Valentich's own account as described in his last six-minute radio conversation with Melbourne Flight Service. (See Page 97)

Vivienne described how it created a silhouette as it moved behind trees, which also adds a certain perspective and substance to the sighting.

It then settled down in the paddock and on departure left a circle of dry, dead grass about fifteen metres in diameter, which they discovered next day. According to Vivienne's account, the grass wasn't burned, but more as if it had died through lack of water.

When Kevin arrived around the front in the car, they both watched it for about twenty minutes before departing to attend the RSL meeting. Curious that they prioritised not being late for the RSL meeting over watching the UFO.

With the benefit of hindsight, Vivienne later acknowledged how illogical this reasoning was, but apparently, one of her colleagues was accusing her of always being late, and for her, that was enough to hold sway.

There were many references in Vivienne's account, including many King Island names during the 1970s who had seen the same type of phenomena and spoken to her about them, and there were also some others who were afraid to speak of their experiences.

It was only as a result of Kevin's passing in 2000 that Vivienne had felt free to talk of her own experience, as Kevin had always been fearful of criticism and wholly against her relating anything about their encounter with the UFO while he was alive.

Vivienne had told me that some encounters on King Island went on for an hour or two and had been witnessed by multiple individuals.

According to Vivienne, one person had gone out duck shooting before dawn but then abandoned the trip, arriving back home in a very shaken emotional state and refusing to go back out again after having an encounter with a UFO, something he couldn't or wouldn't explain.

There was a commonality throughout all the eyewitness accounts, such as the shape of the objects, their speed and their flight patterns. But there was one more aspect that intrigued me as well, being the circles of dead grass that had existed after the craft had departed.

This is a common phenomenon and has been observed by many other people in many other locations around King Island. When Vivienne broached the subject with a neighbouring family of five, everyone immediately stopped talking and "the room went dead quiet".

They then asked her what she had seen, and they all said that they had seen them too, observing these lights for as long as a couple of hours one night. She said she felt they were very affected by their experience.

Respected UFO watcher, the late Paul Norman, also made note of these circles of dead grass at various reported UFO landing sites, but there were many, many others too.

They were observed at the location of the Kettering Incident in southern Tasmania and commonly in the "nest of UFOs" sightings at Tully, Far North Queensland, in 1966.

In 1966, this phenomenon was also famously recorded at Westall, just east of Melbourne. Witnessed in broad daylight by no less than 200 schoolchildren, their teachers and various locals, all of whom were counselled in the days that followed by attending members of the army, air force, police and other uniformed officials.

They were repeatedly warned by the headmaster not to speak to the press or repeat anything of what they had seen other than the official version, that it was nothing more than a collapsed weather balloon. A version of events the witnesses have all absolutely and collectively refuted.

Reportedly, there were three craft sighted at Westall that day. So, would that also indicate that there were three collapsed weather balloons at that location on that day as well?

As a 12-year-old Terry Peck had attended Westall primary school and was there on the 6th of April 1966. I spoke with her at her home in Melbourne.

She told me how she and the other students witnessed something so incredible that day in the form of three visiting UFO's, an experience which lasted for about 20 minutes.

That day she was both witness to the unimaginable and victim to the unforgivable. To the lies bullying and intimidation from those who had held positions of trust and those who had stolen their collective voices. Just like many others, she had chosen not to speak of the event for many years.

She also told me that chemistry teacher Barbara Robins who had taken photos at close quarters of one of the craft that had landed that day at "The Grange", a bushland reserve adjacent to the school, had her camera and film confiscated without cause or explanation.

Neither the camera or its film, which contains vital evidence, and have ever been seen since.

Terry then spoke of seeing the hovering craft turn on its side and move to height at great speed, hover there for a short period in company with the other two craft and then the three of them had literally disappeared.

Not fly off, they had just disappeared.

This is characteristic is not uncommon, as also evidenced later in a statement by Westall's science teacher the late Andrew Greenwood, in Clive's handwritten letter (chapter 13), and by Fred himself over the radio. After having watched the object orbiting above him he had followed up a few seconds later with, "it's just vanished".

Just vanished! An interesting comment coming from him, given that he would have witnessed the craft disappear from his view on various occasions already. But with this statement rather than him having said, "I've lost sight of it" or "I can't see it right now", he says that it had "just vanished", disappeared in front of his very eyes, and I choose to take him entirely at his word. To my knowledge, 48 years after the event, I am the very first to make this critical observation and I also point out that it is highly unlikely Fred could have previously been aware of these unique behavioral characteristics either.

In a witness statement of considerable relevance (ABC news), Andrew Greenwood stated that on the day he'd seen a flying craft that accelerated at "unimaginable speed vertically, disappeared from one spot, turned up in another spot, changed direction, dropped and faded to nothing, then appeared somewhere else".

Such instances have caused speculation that these craft are not travellers through space, but instead, travellers in time. Maybe even from this earth.

By their own admission, the teachers were both individually and collectively threatened with dismissal, blacklisting and even being charged under the Official Secrets Act if they spoke of their experience to the press.

This threat was in itself revealing, as what can justify being charged under the Official Secrets Act if it was only a collapsed meteorological balloon?

According to Westall researcher Shane Ryan on a Studio 10 segment "Melbourne UFO Mystery: 50 Years On" in 2016, witness statements had been made to him by no less than 96 people saying that they had witnessed a flying saucer, and another 147 people saying that they had seen curious and unexplained circles of dead or dry grass at their landing sites.

This lends weight to Vivienne Baldock's testimony as she would have been highly unlikely to have had any knowledge or interest in UFOs or of the unique markings they had left in the grass upon their departure.

These facts taken in isolation are easy to dismiss as a curiosity and "just one of those things", but it is important to maintain some situational awareness and keep an "open mind" when collating the evidence.

Not having any expertise as a UFO watcher per se, I take little interest in them, other than of the encounters I have turned up while investigating the unique circumstances surrounding Fred's own disappearance.

This includes the story of the "Kaikoura Lights" on the east coast of the South Island of New Zealand and of the credible witnesses associated with that event, including our own Quentin Fogarty, anchor for Channel 0 television in Australia at the time.

It is the story of a night freight Argosy aircraft flying along the Kaikoura Coast in and out of Christchurch late one night, and it is compelling viewing.

Confirmed as having also been seen on Christchurch radar, the sighting had occurred on the 21st of December 1978, two months to the day after Fred disappeared. Many references to it can be found on YouTube with film and photos taken by Fogarty from the aircraft that night.

Given the similarity of the objects and the way they moved through space, the connection with Fred's own account is obvious and hard to disregard.

Given also that these sightings on King Island and the Kaikoura Coast occurred at or around the same time as Fred's disappearance and weren't exactly a secret, why weren't they included in the Department of Transport's (DoT) report on the disappearance of Frederick Valentich? Why weren't they flagged by the investigators as having some relevance?

It would be reasonable to expect that they should have been.

I found it to be quite incredible that the investigating authorities, the Bureau of Air Safety Investigation (BASI) as it was known then, thought that it was more important to include Fred's secondary school report in their investigators' notes.

They had also related the fact that Fred was an obsessed UFO watcher.

During the whole course of my investigation, I had found nothing to support the allegation that Fred was an avid UFO watcher.

Was there a wilful campaign to destroy Fred's credibility so that they wouldn't have to deal with the conundrum of a missing aircraft, a missing pilot, and a UFO as the culprit? Or was it simply incompetence that had led to such a lame and botched investigation?

This cassette tape had one other major usefulness for me. It had, hand in hand with my illness, piqued my interest and sent me down this road again, compelling me to delve deeper into this cold case of a missing aviator, 47 years after the event.

It was time to find the energy to get the facts out there in whatever fashion that I could and while I still could.

Sadly, I know of quite a few witnesses associated with this event who have passed away already. Nothing is forever and none of us live forever.

Quentin Fogarty. Passed away 5th of July 2020.

6

I see the man

I don't think there's a soul on this planet who wouldn't do at least something differently if they had a second swing at things. "No regrets" is a romantic saying that to me is just that, a romantic saying.

We all own regrets, but we have all come this far to be just who we are, and that includes all of life's mistakes as well.

It takes a lifetime's experience to form the cognition and comprehension of what is occurring, and to be constructive and to comment with authority on matters at hand.

That's one of the advantages of getting older and it's called wisdom.

In the workplace, it's called professional wisdom.

My career path had been very ad hoc. I have always felt that I hadn't chosen my career path, but that it had chosen me. Beginning with my first flying lessons in Nairobi in 1979 at the end of an overland trip, I had continued with my studies after returning to Australia, more due to a love of seeing the country from the air than to a dedicated love of aeroplanes. For me it was just the natural thing to do.

In that way, my professional destiny as a pilot could well be the retelling of the story of the disappearance of pilot Frederick Valentich with the accumulated knowledge gained over the many years of flying in and out of the little coastal airstrip at Apollo Bay which, over time, has helped me to fill in the historical blanks as best I could.

As the old Catholic nuns who taught me had said, "We all have a calling, and it will be something that sets you apart, something that makes you the best in the world at what you do. It's just a matter of finding it." and for me it has been the writing of this book.

Having gained extensive firsthand knowledge over the years of that location and its geography, including getting to know and interview the various locals who were able to provide eyewitness accounts, I felt a sense of duty to offer my insight into what I think actually occurred that evening.

I speak of the experience gained over 20 years as a chief pilot and of running a business in the often very challenging conditions that are to be encountered around Bass Strait, Cape Otway and King Island, both by day and by night and in all kinds of weather.

Telling this story in whatever fashion, be it an awkward depiction of fact or an award-winning Nobel Prize for literature, which it is safe to say it won't be, isn't at all relevant to the end game.

At the end of the day, it will not only make public what I have come to know about Fred's fate, but also help define my career's end as well.

I have a duty to isolate and relate the facts about Fred's disappearance as clearly and truthfully as I possibly can, and it is apparent to me that fairness and truthfulness have very much been the victim in all the documented analysis that I have hitherto encountered.

Neither is it my intention to deliver a verdict on what became of Fred after the fact; I do, however, hold an informed opinion.

I also intend to assert beyond reasonable doubt that he was always in control of the situation at hand right up until the moment of his disappearance, being very much at odds with the opinions reflected in the official investigators' notes of the day.

As a struggling career pilot, Fred would have had his own mental challenges. This is an area that should also be considered when getting the full picture of what actually occurred. Subtle but important.

I am simply pointing out that Fred had bitten off a lot by working days at the Disposal Store and previously nights at the Astro Bar at Tullamarine Airport while attempting to study five aviation commercial pilot subjects as well.

A nigh on impossible undertaking.

Fred's failure in these subjects was quoted in the investigators' notes as a reason for his supposed depression, and in theory, a possible precipitating factor for him having allegedly taken his own life.

There is something that I would like to bring to the fore as an individual who can call himself qualified to comment on both Fred's capabilities and his disposition, even though I didn't ever know him.

I can wholly sympathise with his circumstances, relating to his record of poor academic achievement as being similar to myself, and subject to the same damaging comments of being incapable of ever achieving passes in commercial pilot theory.

This is where this whole investigation takes a very personal turn. All through Fred's short life, I see parallels with my own life. To me, he was normal.

Suffice to say, the passion for learning to fly was a powerful motivator, both for him and so too for myself.

In all of this, I see the man.

7

An inquiry gone wrong

In a small departure from the task at hand, I would like to reach out in particular to Fred's family, both deceased and remaining, including his fiancée and love of his life, Rhonda Rushton.

To all these people, I extend my deepest condolences, not only for their loss but also for the weight of stress, hurt and humiliation that they had to endure based largely upon irrelevant evidence, discreditation and baseless character assassination relating to Fred.

In 2018, the Australian Transport Safety Bureau (ATSB) responded to me in an email that in effect refused to re-open the case of missing pilot, Frederick Valentich.

It is also apparent to me that nothing has changed in their mindset to this day, despite many recent disclosures about UFO's, the reliability of those reports and the frequency with which they were occurring.

The DoT investigators of the day didn't appear to be exercising any degree of critical thinking, so much so that I was left to question the formality of their investigative skills. Or was it simply that they had no capacity to process the events that had been thrust upon them?

There is no evidence in the aviation investigators' notes of anyone ever having approached the local Apollo Bay police, the Cape Otway Lightstation or Southern Air Services, the establishment where Fred had hired the aircraft. Nor any of the other leading eye witnesses, such as Roy Manifold or Mervyn O'Meara, both well-known names associated with this matter.

There seems to have been no appetite to purposefully expand their lines of inquiry or for anything at all that may have encouraged and prolonged an ongoing debate to do with Fred's disappearance. The lack of response is bewildering.

These oversights were so blatant that one must ask the question: was it incompetence or was it intentional? Or even was it that they were instructed not to?

As far as I can ascertain, as an obvious starting point neither was there any effort in constructively seeking out land-based witnesses for the sightings of conventional aircraft in the vicinity or of UFOs, both on the Australian mainland or on King Island.

It appears that from the very outset, they couldn't properly process the report of a "UFO" being associated with a missing person and a missing aircraft. This remains evident to the current day.

Was there, and is there still, a standing directive not to engage when it comes to discussing evidence, old or new, on matters relating to this case?

It is interesting to note that the 1966 case of Melbourne's famous Westall Incident had triggered a rapid and choreographed response of all the authorities, Police, Army, Air Force and high-level government officials. They had all apparently adopted the same preventative approach of inaction, denial, and of denial with threats.

Justifiably, the internet has its critics, but it has also been credited with uncovering much in the way of truthful recount, and everyone benefits from that.

The assumption on my part has always been that the authorities would like to move on and not have to subject themselves or their agents to too much pain when trying to solve what may in fact be the unsolvable.

That is all on the presumption that they didn't know and have never known anything at all about the existence of UFOs in the Australian airspace.

But conversely, when dissecting their report, one must also consider the not-so-remote possibility that the Australian authorities do know more than they are letting on, and that's why they were and still seem so keen to kill off the possibility of a protracted, transparent inquiry into missing pilot Frederick Valentich.

In 2018, the ATSB also stated to me in an email words to the effect that any information coming forward now cannot be relied upon and that the case was closed in 1982 and will not be re-opened.

This is strange when the primary reason for the existence of the ATSB is for the proper, non-biased reporting and dissemination of relevant information regarding air safety incidents and accidents, without imposing a time limit on those submissions. It is their raison d'être.

So, for me, it's just natural to be suspicious when informed that no further discussion will be entered into.

I am wondering what the response would be if I were to approach the ATSB with information that had come to hand about the disappearance of the now 87-year-old mystery of Amelia Earhart or even that of Malaysian Airlines MH370? Are there time limits on these cases as well?

In fact, case in point with the latter, while we are told things that do not really look good for Captain Zaharie Ahmad Shah of Malaysian Airlines MH370, it could be said that the easiest option is to set him up as being the problem, but by all accounts Captain Zaharie was a man of integrity with a faultless history as a pilot and as a father.

What is the relevance of all this to Fred's disappearance?

In the absence of any hard evidence that would confirm just how either of these aircraft met their end, the pilot is often held to account with assumptions and extrapolations to adversely support that scenario.

Given the amount of effort going into solving the riddle of MH370's disappearance, the truth, whatever it is, will no doubt come out one day, and only after we know all the facts will we then be able to either exonerate or condemn the captain. Only then.

Granted, the circumstances in these disappearances vary considerably. One was a light plane and the other an airliner with 239 souls on board, but it could also be argued that both pilots had just found themselves to be in the wrong place at the wrong time, and both have mysteriously disappeared without cause or reason.

Neither pilot is around to defend their position and to date, neither aircraft has ever been located.

In the case of VH-DSJ, Fred's aircraft, many locals in the Apollo Bay and Cape Otway region either saw the aircraft or a strange light in the sky but were never given the credibility that they deserved, nor were they subsequently even approached for further comment, even after having already tendered preliminary reports about what they had seen that day.

Being the captain of an aircraft has a certain undeniable cache and prestige associated with it. Goes with the job, and rightfully so. But when things go wrong, and in the absence of any conclusive evidence as to the cause of the incident, the captain's actions are often unjustifiably over-scrutinised.

Another case in point was when Captain Chesley Sullenberger landed US Airways Flight 1549 on the Hudson River, New York, in 2009, after multiple bird strikes took out both motors on his Airbus A320, turning the aircraft into a glider over the heavily populated area.

Lives lost: 0

An astounding effort and cool display of professionalism by any account, but true to type, the captain came under scrutiny for his decision-making.

Complex allegations were aired, proven to be baseless and subsequently thrown out, but not before exacting a toll on his personal life.

At the risk of repeating myself, when things go wrong, the pilot in command of an aircraft is a big target.

Fred's last six-minute radio transmission has been heavily scrutinised. He reported unusual aerial activity in his close proximity, but regrettably, he was never actually taken at his word, with just about every other excuse and reason that could be conjured and offered up as a likely cause for his disappearance.

It is obvious to me that the record of his radio transmission should have initially held sway over any other subsequent lines of investigation.

Should that have occurred, it would also have uncovered the plethora of UFO sightings at both Cape Otway and on King Island fifty nautical miles to the south, thus supporting his account of events as related in his last VHF radio conversation with Melbourne Flight Service Officer Steve Robey.

According to a conversation I had with Steve, a professional audio analysis of Fred's voice has been undertaken in America. It was determined that Fred was indeed under stress, meaning he wasn't simply fabricating a false scenario in an attempt to stage his own disappearance.

I have heard the original recording, and it has been a major motivation for me in the writing of this book.

After listening to the tape on multiple occasions, I am of the belief that he was in complete control of his aircraft during his conversation with Melbourne Flight Service.

Through the whole of this book, I have made it plain that I will state the facts as truthfully and as plainly as I see them, but that I won't unreasonably construct answers that are outside of my expertise. Where it is an opinion, I will state it as my opinion.

His last transmission to Melbourne Flight Service, ending a full six minutes before official last light, has subsequently been pulled apart, dissected and positively analysed verbatim by experts without drawing any conclusions other than to come up with the DoT findings that Fred was either delusional or that he was fabricating the encounter. At the end of the day, they gave his eyewitness report zero credit.

In effect, they chose not to believe him.

Notably, what was never mentioned in that transmission was the use of the acronym "UFO" which I think would have been the obvious thing to do if the pilot in this scenario was planning to stage his own disappearance and as a parting gesture leave this world with an enduring mystery.

They can draw no definite conclusions as to what had transpired, and as to what became of the young pilot and his aircraft other than to declare in absentia that his witness and testimony as a pilot stood for nothing.

How incredible is that when you take a minute to think about it?

What constitutes a credible report of a threat to air safety when our investigating authorities subsequently return fire with "No, we think he's most likely suffered from spatial disorientation, no, we think he's possibly suicidal, no, he's possibly absconding with the aircraft, and anyway, we think he's of low IQ, so nothing to see here".

The contemporary term for this, is "gaslighting".

There wasn't one scintilla of effort put into investigating what the pilot had reported, and that was seeing a UFO that tracked him at close quarters and at incredible and threatening speeds.

Psychologists say that not to be believed is an enormously degrading experience for the victim. How much of late have we seen of this to do with abuse?

It turns the victim into the problem and shuts down the conversation, even posthumously, as it did then for Fred.

The victim then becomes the perpetrator. The bad one.

Through all of this, we should never forget that the DoT had previously granted Fred his flying licence but then were quick to call him out, questioning his IQ and insinuating that he wasn't at all fit to hold that licence.

Conversely, these criticisms don't make them look too good either as the initial issuer of that same licence.

A word-of-mouth report from a reliable source was that none other than Jacques Cousteau, the famous French submariner, had offered to come out to Australia in his vessel *Calypso* and sweep Bass Strait with state-of-the-art sonar in an extraordinary effort to hopefully locate the aircraft wreck, but that the Australian Government had not supported it.

Again. If that report is true, and I was assured that it was, then one must ask why not, when it would have been, or at least could have been privately funded?

Certainly, the controversy would have continued for a lot longer had that occurred and perhaps that wasn't what the decision makers wanted to happen.

A possible reason that the enquiry was being shut down was that the government authority was aware of UFO activity occurring in a lot of locations and acted in keeping with the old-style paternalistic mentality of the day: control the population by controlling the information and manipulating the truth.

It's not an illogical conclusion and the Westall Incident in 1966 was a perfect example. A certain Australian ally has already got form in this regard.

Given the more recent, transparent and credible UFO sightings around the globe and other emerging credible reports of non-human technology and alien bodies being held deep within the secret enclaves of an American "dark administration", it would be reason enough to assume that the ATSB could have been more sympathetic to any new submission on the subject of the Valentich disappearance.

This prospect no longer seems so farfetched, with leading figures such as Democratic Senator for New York Chuck Schumer and Republican Senator for South Dakota Mike Rounds in July 2023 throwing their bipartisan weight behind groundbreaking congressional legislation into the need to declassify records related to extraterrestrial encounters.

Promises have also been recently made by the Trump administration as we await their honesty and candour on the topic of UFOs and other associated documentation with support growing for yet more congressional hearings, which are now occurring.

This includes many things, but primarily that NHI is being held in secret archives and protected by legislation originally enacted by President Dwight D. Eisenhower in 1954. In so doing, it also assesses the threat that UAPs may pose to the security of the United States of America.

Just as a side note, how on earth does legislation such as the 1954 Eisenhower legislation get to have life breathed into it?

Who writes it, and what governing authority ultimately presides over both its existence and its enforcement? If it's not the president of the elected government, then who?

We should be more than just concerned, and this is a good example as to why.

These are the questions that have come to be front of mind when investigating the events surrounding the disappearance of a lost and forgotten airman from my hometown.

It is alleged that the specimens referred to in the above amendment to the National Defense Authorisation Act (NDAA) have been secretly held for decades in top-secret American vaults, far pre-dating the disappearance of Frederick Valentich in 1978.

Also, following that line of thinking, whoever it was that made the call to derail the investigation into Fred's disappearance did so due to the reported involvement of a UFO and the part it had played in that incident.

That call could well have come from other shores and I'm suspecting that it had.

In this way, Fred could have found himself to be a casualty of something far bigger than he could have ever imagined. Something that stretched all the way across the globe.

If this is true, then it's quite probable that the Australian Government could have been advised at the highest level by perhaps, just saying, the United States Government at the time, or at least, furtive but influential forces within that government, to both scuttle the inquiry and to pour cold water on anything that would prolong public debate in the newssheets of the day.

They certainly had with the Westall Incident in 1966.

Given my understanding of human nature, the most effective way to attack Fred's credibility was to simply question his mental health or his IQ level, especially so in those days when poor mental health carried with it a certain stigma and was treated by society at large as a profound weakness of character.

Where do we stop with all of this? And it also raises the question of other reports or documents that we weren't allowed to view. To put it another way, are they revealing all there is to know about the Valentich case?

It's the old story: when trust is gone, then it's hard to regain, and born out of a growing suspicion, all possibilities are then back on the table.

If I am correct, if the instruction was to close this investigation down, or at best hobble it by employing a discrete program of discreditation, then that to me is anti-democratic. It is against the charter of our elected public servants, being more akin to the policy of a communist regime.

It is corruption.

I wondered what had been so apparently wrong with this pilot that had precipitated such a swathe of criticism, not only in the public eye, but also from that of the flying community at large.

In such controversial circumstances, Fred was a huge target and without anyone to speak up in his defence, investigative reports were of a random nature, often very personal, often completely off point and without any relevance to solving the riddle of a missing person.

This was particularly apparent in the record of the interview of Fred's fiancée, Rhonda Rushton, and the relevance of the deeply personal line of questioning that the interviewers had adopted.

In her own words, it was both intimidating and overbearing. It was one that she had attended as a 16-year-old girl, alone and without representation.

It is worth mentioning a confusing and implausible statement included in the file on the interview with Rhonda. It states that Rhonda had to wipe Fred's brow when he was under pressure and that Fred, at one point, had to make a number of attempts to land the aircraft when she had flown with him.

This record has been wholly refuted by Rhonda, stating to me in an email in 2018 that she didn't know where it had emanated from and that it was completely untrue.

This email is a critical response from Rhonda referring to the typed DoT interview notes between herself, a 16-year-old girl and the DoT, three days after Fred's disappearance. I refer to it on multiple occasions.

Of interest to me as a pilot was the fact that in the very same paragraph was also stated that the "reason Valentich couldn't land the plane was that the control column was locked".

To anyone who knows anything about aircraft, this is quite a fantastic claim and does more to question the investigators' competency than that of the pilot who was under scrutiny.

It is absolutely impossible to fly an aircraft in any phase of flight with a control lock engaged.

Fred's failure to pass the Air Force entrance exam was also used as a reason to discredit him when in reality it is a very difficult exam to pass. I knew many who didn't pass it and then subsequently turned to the airlines as a career choice and were ultimately successful.

My perspective is that references made to Fred's secondary school academic qualifications in the official file report were irrelevant and appeared to be downright vindictive. Cowardly references to his prowess and low skill level as a pilot and to his general IQ were totally unproven, baseless and irrelevant in the case of a missing-person investigation.

They do, however, serve one purpose, and that is to question the motive of the investigating team.

This was meant to be an investigation into an aviation incident involving a missing person, not an end-of-term school report.

Italian was the primary language spoken in the family home and whilst today there would be tolerance for this with even a chance of turning it into a positive, not so then. It would have been a hindrance to Fred's academic advancement within a rigid education system.

In this way poor school reports were merely symptomatic, the environment must be right for a mind to flourish.

At this point, I would like to wade in on one of the more controversial matters surrounding Fred's personality: that of his alleged propensity to mark himself up when in fact he hadn't achieved passes at all in the relevant subjects, and this, from what I can determine, had been used to challenge his mental stability.

Rhonda freely admits that very early in their relationship, Fred had lied to her by misrepresenting the truth of his exam results, but that they had a big talk and he had admitted to doing this and he had promised to never deceive her again.

Can't this just be regarded as a healthy development in a developing young relationship rather than an indication of something more sinister?

During our lives, who among us has not found it difficult to relate the absolute truth when called upon to do so under pressure?

For whatever reason, Fred, new at the game, did not appear to be aware of his own limitations with respect to ground school. Call it impatience, impetuousness or just plain zeal, but Fred bit off a lot more than he or anyone else could chew when it came to tackling his aviation theory subjects.

As I have already said, sitting five subjects at once and working full-time is an impossible undertaking and is more a reflection of his unrealistic grip on reality than of his aptitude.

At times, I had also confidently predicted that I had passed a certain Commercial Pilot Licence (CPL) or ATPL subject, only to receive an abrupt wakeup call when the mail arrived. In those days, it was hardcopy, which seemed to make it even worse in some ways.

According to Rhonda, this is also what had occurred with Fred. He had anticipated passes, but unfortunately, when the results arrived, that wasn't the case. On one occasion, Fred had even bought two bottles of wine in advance to share with Rhonda and his Air Force friend and study support person, Bob Barnes.

Bob had advised him not to open them until he actually had the results in his hand. According to Rhonda, the bottles had remained unopened.

Call it hubris or exuberance, emotions run high when you think that you're on the other side of those exams, and while you really want to believe that you are, reality can ultimately be extremely deflating. I, too, had learnt the hard way and not to be so naïvely optimistic.

Rhonda said that she thought Fred had underestimated the exam's degree of difficulty and that he was "ok" after he had a taste of reality.

This sort of thing often happened not only to myself and Fred but to many of the other CPL and ATPL students that I transited ground school with.

The investigators had overemphasised this whole scenario, implying that Fred wasn't in touch with reality and as a result, was possibly mentally unstable.

They inferred this could indicate a predisposition for him to end his own life by staging an encounter with a UFO or by flying off to parts unknown.

Tragic thoughts if they were true, but I still think it is a very long bow to draw over failed theory subjects given all the positives in Fred's life, which cannot be ignored when having this conversation.

I have been told that Fred's father, Guido, was naturally proud of Fred's chosen career, but my senses also tell me that, in his desire to please, there would also have been expectations that weighed heavily on his young shoulders.

I'm not an expert on mental health but I would argue that the investigators hadn't exhibited any special qualities in that direction either, or that perhaps they themselves were the ones who were in need of a reality check.

It is reasonably apparent that there was a subcurrent of unjustified discreditation throughout the whole DoT report to do with Fred's disappearance, something that I'm sure would not have occurred at all had a UFO not figured so prominently in the whole affair.

For BASI, it could have been the easier way of closing down a controversial aviation incident report for which there was no known answer. More to the point, it is evident there didn't even seem to be any expertise to satisfactorily head up the inquiry.

The only report that I have seen about the one and only aircraft component ever recovered that was purportedly from VH-DSJ was that of a cowl flap from the lower forward fuselage of the engine cowl. This somewhat flat rectangular aluminium component measures about 300 mm by 200 mm and its job is to either warm or cool the engine by being manually opened and closed by the pilot.

It was found on the beach about five years later at Flinders Island, which is in the Furneaux Group of islands on the east side of Bass Strait, three hundred kilometres away from where Fred went missing.

It wasn't able to be successfully matched by the serial number which, except for a prefix, was incomplete.

The Cessna 182 is a four seat, high wing bush aircraft commonly used on the challenging airstrips of Flinders Island and the Furneaux Group.

To think that a non-buoyant aluminium component would migrate 300 kilometres along the ocean floor, even accounting for ocean currents, is optimistic at the very least. According to the report, the part had also been repainted with an acrylic paint that was inconsistent with the paint used on VH-DSJ.

Also, judging by the photos, there was absolutely no evident sign of barnacle or weed growth on the component that would be consistent with five years immersed in the ocean.

Perhaps that growth had been removed, and if so, then vital evidence will have been destroyed, and with it much that could have been determined by the age and the species of the barnacles. Again, this speaks loudly of the lack of expertise of those conducting the investigation.

Although there are a number of pages covering this component in the official report, I think it would be safe to disregard this cowl flap as evidence in the disappearance.

A separate note from an investigator on the team referred to a light in the evening sky that Fred may have seen and mistaken to be a UFO: "Venus was very bright in the sky that evening too …"

Despite this whole scenario being quite fantastic and highly unlikely as a factor in Fred's disappearance for a lot of reasons, on that night Venus was visible in the night sky on a bearing of 255 degrees and Fred's track at that point was 155 degrees magnetic. That's a difference of 100 degrees.

It would have barely been in his field of view and most likely unnoticeable, concealed behind the right hand side wing of his high wing Cessna aircraft.

However you look at it, this is a desperate attempt on their behalf to find answers and I'm going to let this one just slide right through to the keeper.

Yet another investigator's note said that there was reportedly a plague of moths in the Cape Otway area which at altitude may have been responsible for creating an illusion and also could have affected the aircraft's engine air intake, resulting in a reduction in engine power.

Seriously?

No words.

In summary, I will first refer back to Fred's experience level of somewhere between 150 and 200 flight hours. It is impossible to exactly determine, and with the benefit of my years and exposure to the circumstances of the incident, I will say why he needs to be, where possible, exonerated from any allegations of poor airmanship vis-à-vis being that he was flying under the effects of spatial disorientation. This will be discussed in detail in chapter 10.

The investigators' preliminary report also noted that Fred chose to leave the microphone on his lap where it rested between his legs during periods of non-use. I'm not at all sure why, but it was written up as something irregular in the investigators' notes.

This was in the day before it was the accepted norm for pilots to own and wear their own headphones. Many didn't own headphones and spoke to Flight Service and other aircraft using the handheld microphone and a speaker in the roof of the aircraft which would have done nothing to obviate aircraft engine and propeller noise.

No doubt this would account for the substandard sound recording of Fred's voice in the final radio conversation with Flight Service Officer Steve Robey.

I didn't own headphones in those days myself and when the pressure was on, I also used to leave the microphone in my lap during periods of high usage. It made for quick access and it was just common sense.

The night after the disappearance of Frederick Valentich, crayfish fisherman and born-and-bred Apollo Bay local Mark Garrett had arrived home in his boat from King Island with a load of crayfish. Turning on the TV, he saw that he and his boat *The Vanguard* were on the evening news after having been filmed from a news aircraft.

The report went on to add that *The Vanguard* was part of the seconded civilian fleet involved in the search for the missing pilot Frederick Valentich.

This was the source of some amusement according to Mark, as neither he nor the crew had known anything about the disappearance until that moment.

More than a simple reporter error, and in no way connected to the official investigators' efforts, it is perhaps a glimpse of the need to fuel a hungry media's appetite for any news to do with a UFO and a missing aircraft, factual or otherwise.

This included a headline report in one major Australian newspaper stating that Rhonda had travelled to Apollo Bay a week after the disappearance to secretly rendezvous with Fred. While obviously untrue, by her own admission, this had caused her much anxiety and stress but was by no means an isolated incident.

The air search itself was described to me as being somewhat haphazard and random, perhaps typical of the day. To be fair, search-and-rescue capabilities in that era were very underdeveloped and are not a reflection of our current response effectiveness, which is world's best practice.

At the 11th hour, I was made aware of an article posted online in 'Flight Safety' dated February 2025…just seven months ago.

In their own words, Flight Safety is CASAs flagship safety magazine. In a rambling delivery, it revealed their (CASA's) official position on the reasons for the disappearance of Frederick Valentich have, for the past 47 years remained unchanged.

Lacking depth or analysis they speculate that Fred's disappearance is likely a result of him having either, suffered from a suicidal tendency combined with a preoccupation with UFOs and the influence of cognitive bias (seeing what one wants to see contrary to the facts as they are presented), after having been deceived by the illusion of Venus in the night sky. Or that he had suffered from the effects of spatial disorientation; all at once and without proper cause or reasoning.

Strikes me no one is immune from the effects of cognitive bias, including the investigators.

In an unjustified and condescending summation of what probably would've been Fred's career path in Aviation, it concludes with, and I quote:

"Had Valentich not disappeared, he may have been about now coming to the end of a long aviation career, perhaps in cabin crew, engineering, airport operations or ground handling. Like many of us who fall in love with Aviation, he may have with maturity, come to accept that his role in the system would involve his feet staying firmly on the ground, but would be no less vital because of this".

Not forgetting they were the ones who had granted Fred his flying licence together with a class 4 instrument rating in the first place.

While the subject of Fred's failure in his commercial pilot ground school subjects remain contentious, my assessment (see next chapter) is that it is most likely the result of overload, but without the foundation of a full and proper investigation this all has no bearing on answering the big questions, what actually occurred that night and could Fred have been telling the truth?

Overall, this view seems consistent with their old policy of gaslighting and discreditation, constituting an unreasonably harsh posthumous assessment on the ability and character of a young pilot who is not here to defend himself.

It seems nothing has changed, and it justifies a major premise of this book.

8

Headwinds

Fred was struggling to achieve passes in his commercial ground school subjects while holding down a full-time day job as a storeman at the Army Disposals as well as attending day school. Up until June 1978, he had also been employed working nights at The Astro Bar at Tullamarine Airport.

On top of that, he had attempted five subjects all at once when it was more common practice to sit only one or maybe two at a time, even if you weren't working full-time.

A herculean task by any account.

Why he took on so much isn't clear, but possibly there was pressure from home and the need to show that he was making headway. Or was it even just impatience?

University courses for CPL and ATPL didn't exist, and it isn't drawing too long a bow to say that in low-income, working-class Australia, "Tall Poppy Syndrome" flourished.

The announcement of such a career choice could have been seen as tantamount to grandstanding among the general working-class population, where air travel was regarded as a luxury and employment within its ranks a privilege.

Was this also a contributing factor for Fred to bite off more than he could chew in an effort to prove himself, coming from the working-class suburb of Avondale Heights in Melbourne's outer west?

These days, the government HECS scheme and the universities offer a far more workable, sustainable and stable approach to the choice of a career as a commercial pilot. It would be fair to say that back in Fred's and my day, becoming an "airline pilot" was an informal and unusual career choice and that there was very little government support, if any.

The commercial air pilot's examination subjects were and still are very difficult to pass. Failures, sometimes multiple failures, weren't uncommon. There was no disgrace in failing and re-sitting.

Many did, I did, and it's fair to say that too much emphasis during the investigation had been placed upon Fred's aviation subject track record, because I suspect it suited someone to use that record for all the wrong reasons.

Courses were relatively short and intense, and it was generally recognised that immediately reviewing the recent class material while it was still fresh in your head was always the most productive and positive way of absorbing the subject matter.

It's quite apparent that this wasn't a luxury that Fred could ever afford for himself and not allocating that time was seen as the road to failure, despite his best intentions. Anyone who has been through this will agree that it is imperative to keep your head in that space during that period.

Even the "easy" subjects required focus and commitment. IQ alone was not the determining factor in establishing success.

The Department of Transport (later Civil Aviation Safety Authority, CASA) did nothing to ameliorate the situation. The perception of the day among candidates was that the authority was often, rightly or wrongly, regarded as being obstructive to that end. This was most apparent in theory exams.

Part of the problem was and still is that the syllabus set by the managing authority was widely criticised by candidates as being irrelevant and out of date.

Reports of exams set by unqualified personnel existed both then and now, but complaints fell on deaf ears.

Ross was someone who knew Fred well, having studied and later worked with him at SAS as a new instructor in the late 1970s.

Later in his career, between 1998 and 2008, he ran the Qantas cadet program. He doesn't speak kindly of CASA and the way they run their exam system, having lobbied them hard for change through the universities and also through Qantas. But on this subject, they had remained intransigent.

He named one examiner who wrote the ATPL (heavy jet, airline grade) exams but who hadn't even attained an initial pass in those subjects himself.

As there was no university degree or HECS funding available, if you chose flying as a career, then you had to fund it yourself by whatever means.

To gain your CPL, you then took it upon yourself to go to the airports and visit the various flying establishments to garner knowledge on how to bring it all together and to make it a reality.

This included the ground school which would often be undertaken at night in some rented room on an airport or even in a lecturer's home. I had to do exactly that.

As a self-employed person, being able to allocate my time as required, I was in a much stronger position than Fred and I had found it difficult enough to achieve passes in these subjects.

Fred was enrolled in John Mansell-Smith's ground school, which was one of the more respected, well-established, ground schools located upstairs in the Schutt Flying Services office loft at Moorabbin Airport. But that wasn't enough to get him over the line with his unrealistic workload and study regime.

The exam questions were supposedly based on psychology and the apparent need to set a high standard, ostensibly to keep the skies safe and protect the fare-paying passenger, but exams were full of questions with double entendre and ambiguity, more reliant upon interpretation rather than a candidate's technical competency.

Outdated textbooks and an outdated syllabus are the same today as they were in Fred's time.

I was reminded of this about five years ago when my son sat for his Restricted Private Pilot's (RPL) theory exam at Moorabbin Airport.

When he came out of the examination, he appeared obviously crestfallen and dejected. He asked me how many hours a pilot was legally allowed to work before a rest break. Of course, they are known as pilot "duty times" and are the times that a professional commercial pilot is bound to by legislation to avoid fatigue in the workplace.

They have no relevance whatsoever to a restricted private licence, but there were questions on that topic in his exam.

Unbeknown to us the home study theory in the book he used at the time, which I shall not name, was not relevant to the syllabus set by CASA. He wasted a lot of time and effort studying the wrong syllabus!

He failed the exam.

Naturally, over the period I had followed his progress, and I was satisfied that he had completed the required amount of study and also that he was across all the syllabus subject matter as presented in that correspondence course, but he still wasn't able to attain a pass in RPL.

Putting this into perspective, he gained an ATAR (Australian Tertiary Administration Rank) score of 99% the following year in his year 12 exam, being his final year at secondary college.

This is the demanding world that Fred had entered in his chosen career as an airline pilot dealing with the relevant authority, the DoT who were completely untouchable on this contentious issue.

This is very relevant when discussing how the investigators chose to headline Fred's failure rate in aviation ground school theory, cruelly and falsely flagging it as a weakness of character, alluding to it as a possible reason for suicide.

Seeing themselves as the guardians of the skies is one thing, but to that end, it is their own competency that should come into focus after having been called upon to uncover the truth of a missing pilot.

In lieu of being able to qualify as a civilian commercial airline pilot, Fred had joined the Air Training Corps in an attempt to find a new direction for his career, together with the security the Air Force could afford him, including a formal academic environment.

It makes sense to me why this path may have been attractive to Fred, as perhaps he saw it as a way of leaving the home environment and gaining independence.

Fred's flying colleague and friend, Ross, had discussed the move with him in terms of what the Air Training Corps could ultimately offer him as a career path but found that his responses were unrealistic.

Fred had seen the Air Force as the way forward, when in reality Ross thought that it was doubtful, and that the move may not have been in the best interests of his career.

It appears that Fred had found something more than flying in the Air Force environment; he'd found another family and wouldn't allow himself to be swayed.

For any chance of the truth of Fred's disappearance to be uncovered, an impartial and competent investigator was needed to head up the enquiry, and he didn't have that.

While Fred attained passes in some CPL subjects, in aviation vernacular, it's fair to say that he had encountered "headwinds" all around, both prior to and subsequent to his disappearance.

9

The flight plan and the flight

Fred's motivation for flying to King Island on the evening of Saturday the 21st has been heavily scrutinised and is surrounded by controversy, insomuch as the reasons he gave for making the trip aren't quite apparent. But he could hardly have ever been aware of the controversy that would subsequently surround the various innocent actions and conversations he had made just prior to his departure.

Typically, nothing is secret when thrust into the public eye through controversy, and what are generally normal conversations and events then become open to unwarranted public scrutiny and critical analysis after the fact.

Had this standard flight gone to plan, and there was absolutely nothing to suggest that it wasn't going to go to plan, then it would have been very much business as usual – one of perhaps hundreds of such flights that occurred without incident around Australia that weekend and many weekends since.

While uncovering the purpose for undertaking the flight may be relevant in shedding some light on the investigation, it is also important to note that a flight plan had been lodged and at face value, there was nothing out of the ordinary or illegal about the flight at all.

Runway lights had not been requested for a landing at King Island but this could have been an oversight or a misunderstanding, given that he had originally planned to arrive during daylight hours. Or even that Fred had later decided to overfly the King Island airport and return to Moorabbin Airport at night using the privileges afforded to him under his recently achieved Class 4 instrument rating.

He was holding plenty of fuel on board to safely complete the return flight. I will analyse this in detail later in the chapter.

While the reason for failing to request lights has never been established, it is important to keep in mind that it is a flight he would have been relatively comfortable with, and one he had previously undertaken three or four times in daylight hours.

The investigators' report mentioned that Fred's father, Guido, had intended to go on the flight but Rhonda refutes that in her 2018 email. It is another of the many inaccuracies of that report.

Fred apparently carried four lifejackets, saying that he intended to pick up passengers for the return leg from King Island. There was no proof of this, but it is known that previously he had randomly offered stranded passengers a lift back to the mainland, not forgetting it was originally planned that, besides himself, his fiancee Rhonda would be using one other of those jackets.

For obvious reasons, flying crayfish in SAS aircraft was prohibited and it wouldn't be unreasonable to assume that Fred was using the excuse of picking up passengers to cover his tracks.

It was stated in the investigators' notes that Fred had "unofficial discussions" with Squadron Leader Ronald Grandy to purchase crayfish for the officers' mess at Point Cook where he was in the Air Training Corps. In fact, Rhonda had seen Ronald give Fred $200 cash to buy crayfish for the planned gathering to be held at the Grandy household on that Saturday evening "if they were available".

Despite the investigators' notes stating that there wasn't any evidence of Fred having pre-ordered crayfish, his intention could well have been to check on their availability after landing using the public telephone box at the airport.

The original plan was that Rhonda was to accompany Fred on the flight to King Island that day, but delays for both of them had changed all that.

The appealing thing for Fred would be that he would begin logging all-important solo night hours and, quite possibly, this had then become his main motivation for continuing with his plans to complete the flight.

Previously, I have stated that both Fred's and my paths are similar and I continually find it hard to separate myself from the events of his life without making comparisons.

My first solo "Nav" as a fresh private pilot was down to Flinders Island in the Furneaux Group of islands in Bass Strait, departing from Tooradin, Victoria. It is an island on the northeast end of the tip of Tasmania and Bass Strait, whereas King Island lies at the western end of Bass Strait.

Both islands lie on the 40th Parallel, marking the northern boundary of the "Roaring Forties" wind zone. It is a region renowned for its high winds and inclement weather but in many ways, the Flinders Island flight is more demanding than the King Island flight.

The day I arrived at the airfield, I was informed by my instructor Glenn Balas, that the weather was questionable and that my companion of the day had pulled out and did I still want to go?

I was to meet up with my old friend Tom Jubb who at the time, held a lease on an island in the Furneaux Group, of which Flinders Island was a part. I was excited at the prospect of a Bass Strait crossing and so cancelling wasn't an option. I feel sure that it would have been exactly the same for Fred that evening as well.

Such excursions as a new pilot were pure adventure and, in all honesty, being "wired" for the experience meant he was going to go anyway, Rhonda or no Rhonda, crayfish or no crayfish.

The fact remains that little can be deduced about Fred's mental state by scrutinising the facts presented regarding his motivation for undertaking the flight, and it is equally hard to establish any premise of intentional self-harm based upon his reason for undertaking it.

A young person quite often does not prioritise reasoning or personal safety when in search of adventure, and it is apparent to me that Fred was typically that type of young person.

Moving forward, no investigation could be complete without the formality of scrutinising the flight plan that was lodged by Fred in person at the Moorabbin Flight Service office on the afternoon of the 21st of October 1978.

According to the available records, the officer on duty that evening was Mr Darcy Hogan.

Fred was the holder of an Unrestricted Private Pilot's Licence and Class 4 Instrument Rating authorising night flight under VFR (Visual Flight Rules) in VMC (Visual Meteorological Conditions). In layman's terms, the privilege of this licence allowed him to pilot an aircraft on a clear night.

The flight plan was for aircraft callsign Victor Hotel-Delta Sierra Juliet (VH-DSJ), Cessna 182L, Moorabbin–King Island (land), King Island–Moorabbin. Planned flight time 147 minutes return. True Air Speed 135 knots.

Weather: 15-knot north-westerly winds, light mid-level cloud and no significant cloud below 5000 feet AMSL.

Visibility excellent.

According to the records Fred had departed Moorabbin Airport at 18:19 and reported Cape Otway at 19:00 local time, a sector time of 41 minutes. Given that the flight planned track distance for this sector was 92 nautical miles, this then results in an actual groundspeed of 135 knots. Exactly as flight planned.

This confirms that the winds that evening were as forecast, 340 degrees magnetic at 15 knots. Establishing this is important.

According to the format of the flight plan, a landing at King Island had been planned. The investigators' notes stated that runway lights had not been requested. This would later become a contentious point.

Fred had originally planned to arrive at Currie, King Island, before last light but he had been unexpectedly delayed for reasons explained later. As a result, his amended ETA for arrival at King Island was after last light and so runway lights would have been a requirement if a landing was to be undertaken.

Also, according to investigators' notes, the attending Flight Service Officer on the island that evening was a Mr Brian Jones who had been on duty from 08:00 until 15:00. Because no aircraft were inbound or had booked runway landing lights for later that evening, he had put in a request to Melbourne to close early, and reportedly this request had been granted.

Rightly or wrongly, there seemed to have been an acceptance on Fred's part that he should proceed as planned with his intentions to land at King Island.

This is supported in his response to Flight Service Officer Steve Robey's question during their final six-minute radio conversation when he asked, "What are your intentions?" to which Fred responded, "My intentions are to go to King Island." In this instance, the intention to "go to King Island" could be interpreted as undertaking a landing at King Island.

VH-DSJ departed Melbourne's Moorabbin Airport with full fuel which in that aircraft was 84 US gallons (318 litres). At an effective cruise fuel flow of 13 US gallons (49 litres) per hour, it would result in an endurance of 389 minutes or approximately six and a half hours.

This was plenty of fuel considering that the total legal fuel requirement for the Moorabbin–King Island return flight was 193 minutes according to Fred's flight plan, which included a 45-minute reserve.

The forecast was good, with no requirement to carry extra "alternate" or "holding" fuel due to adverse weather conditions when returning to Moorabbin. So this was all that was legally required to complete the "private" category flight on the night given the light north-westerly winds and clear skies that had prevailed throughout the region.

Back in the 1980s, I had gained my initial multi-engine instrument rating at Canberra airport with the late Ben Hoitink, a well-respected instructor and gentleman in the industry.

When taxiing the twin engine Beechcraft Baron for the active runway at Canberra and the tower had confirmed that an "intersection departure" was available (meaning a departure from the point where the runways intersect was available to save time), Ben calmly said to me over the aircraft's intercom, "The runway behind and the sky above is of absolutely no use," meaning if the extra runway length is available for take-off, then why not make use of it?

No different for Fred that day when it came to making a decision on how much fuel to carry to take full advantage of all his available options. If the fuel capacity is available, then it's logical to make use of it.

It is generally accepted that providing weight and balance and aircraft gross weight considerations were within limits, when undertaking a flight such as this, pilots would always elect to carry the extra fuel. If the capacity is there, use it. A bit like pulling on an extra blanket.

In my experience, no one elects to fly anywhere on legal minimum fuel unless it's unavoidable. Especially at night. Plus, there was one other advantage: filling an aircraft to capacity obviates the need to do bothersome fuel calculations compared to when the tanks are less than full.

Full fuel is full fuel, a known quantity, and if I were Fred that day, I would have definitely opted to also carry the extra fuel for the flight. However you choose to look at it, it is just good airmanship.

According to the flight plan that was lodged on the day, there was a planned fuel margin of 196 minutes after any reserves, more than double what was legally required for the flight that evening. But when planning to conduct a night flight and for the reasons I have already explained, I would consider this to be completely normal.

I have gone to the trouble of explaining this in some detail to dispel any suggestion Fred had elected to carry full fuel in an attempt to fly as far as he could, for as long as he could in an effort to simply disappear, as has been alleged.

It is an unreasonable and unfair assertion and by far the very least believable of all scenarios.

As the old pilot's adage goes, "fuel equals options", though sadly not for Fred. Not that night.

Minimal information had been entered on the fuel section of the flight plan, giving a total endurance of 193 minutes of fuel required for the return flight, including reserves.

Fred had noted on the flight plan that he was holding 300 minutes endurance when in fact he had, according to my calculations, 389 minutes endurance. Considerably more.

When I asked Ross about this inconsistency, he replied that as far as he was concerned, it wasn't uncommon in the day to generalise for a "private" category flight using a conservative number like "300 minutes" recognising the actual endurance was much higher anyway.

To further confuse the issue, 300 minutes is coincidentally the endurance of the "standard size" 65 US gallon (246 litre) tank in that aircraft but a receipt issued by Mr Ron Tyson of Tysons Refuelling Moorabbin stated that 247 litres had been uploaded into DSJ prior to departure that day, which can be seen is exactly the same total capacity of the "small tanks" in that model aircraft.

During the course of my inquiry, I had noted that there had been some uncertainty about the size of the fuel tanks in DSJ. This, however, confirms that DSJ had been fitted with the "long range" tanks of 84 US gallons (318 litres) as it is implausible that this refuelling would have been on tanks that were completely empty after being flown earlier that day by Mr V. Alphonso, according to available flight records.

For the record, the DoT's own Accident Investigation report stated that DSJ had a total fuel capacity of 318 litres, but in the light of other information in that report, it is worthy of cross-checking.

Re-establishing the known and accepted facts of what had occurred that day pertaining to the planned rendezvous between Fred and Rhonda is essential.

Fred was late getting airborne at Moorabbin Airport after Rhonda had been delayed leaving work, and it is assumed that he would have gone to the local McDonald's to have dinner to wait for her.

The report had included what could only be described as a contrived description of Fred's eating habits, stating that he would have eaten "two Big Macs, two Cheeseburgers, a Filet-O-Fish and some chips and a carton of Coca Cola", an enormous meal and something that Rhonda politely described in her 2018 email to me as bullshit.

The point in mentioning this is to illustrate the reasoning and accuracy of the report, that it is useless information, that isn't even correct, and that it is of no consequence when considered in the light of a missing person's report.

It is hard to imagine in this age of connectivity, but communications in those days were problematic, which would have made coordination between himself and Rhonda difficult, with one investigator's note saying that they had originally planned to depart as early as 16:00 local time.

It is a matter of record that they had agreed to meet up at Moorabbin Airport and that Rhonda would accompany Fred on the flight, but that unexpected delays on both of their parts had changed those plans and that Fred had eventually departed alone.

As evidenced in the inquiry notes and the general flying community at large, the theory was that Fred was depressed and even suicidal as a result of his inability to pass his commercial flying exams and that on that day, he had planned to end his own life or to disappear by flying off to parts unknown.

If any credence is to be given to the theory that Fred was planning his own disappearance or demise, it would also follow that he had originally intended to undertake this dark act with the love of his life Rhonda onboard the aircraft as well. It is an accepted fact that Rhonda was to accompany Fred on the flight that day, but the rendezvous had never happened due to circumstances beyond his control, and so this plan had never come to fruition.

When considering all the facts as they appear, the act of attempted murder-suicide is a perfectly reasonable hypothesis and one that must be considered or at least should have been considered by the investigators if they had been doing their job. It would have been a logical progression in the sequence of events and a prospect that should have at least been aired when working on the assumption that Fred had in fact committed suicide that day.

But connecting all the circumstances of that day would then result in giving Fred a completely new personality, a new modus operandi, based solely upon speculation.

If he had been planning the horrific act of a murder-suicide, and there is absolutely no evidence to support such a theory other than circumstantial, then why wouldn't he have simply postponed the flight for another time when he would have been assured of achieving his objective?

Why wouldn't there have been any warning signs of this in his character that would have conclusively led investigators down that path?

There were none and there have been none, even to this day.

The answer is simple. He wasn't planning to do anything so sinister or horrendous at all that day.

Either in company or alone.

Only a week prior, Fred had bought Rhonda a friendship ring, secretly proposing marriage. The ring was for her to hold as a symbol of his love, commitment and honourable intentions until their official engagement.

Also, in keeping with his ritual of buying her a present for their monthly anniversary, Fred had purchased a hairdryer and presented it to her on Friday, the day before the flight.

An innovative and thoughtful gesture in those days and if Fred was planning to proceed with the ghastly act of murder-suicide, then surely it would be completely at odds with his actions in gifting Rhonda the hairdryer on the very previous day.

It is obvious he was simply fixated on completing his first solo night navigation exercise as pilot in command under the rules of Limited IFR category (Limited Instrument Flight Rules), an exciting prospect for a young pilot and as a secondary priority, perhaps buy some crayfish and be back in time for drinks at Ronald Grandy's house with Rhonda that evening.

Nothing more.

If all had gone to plan and they had departed Moorabbin Airport together and on time, they would have arrived at King Island before last light and so would not have needed to arrange landing lights for landing at the destination. Logically, he would have arranged lights for his departure while on the ground at King Island.

Fred's Estimated Time of Departure (ETD) on his flight plan was 07:45 GMT (Greenwich Mean Time or "Zulu" time as it was commonly called then) or 17:45 local time. This was most likely the latest time that he had calculated to depart Moorabbin and be able to safely undertake a landing at King Island without the use of lights.

However, for reasons unknown, his actual departure time was 34 minutes later, at 18:19 local time.

As noted on his flight plan, if he had he departed at 17:45 as planned, his arrival time overhead King Island would have been 18:59, calculated by adding his flight planned sector time of 69 minutes cruise plus a five-minute allowance for climb, to 17:45. That is a full 19 minutes prior to designated last light at 19:18, ample time to safely conduct a circuit and land. Although this schedule is tight, it is a completely realistic one if everything had gone to plan.

That didn't happen and had he completed the flight leg that night, the delay of 34 minutes would have placed him overhead the airfield at King Island 15 minutes after designated last light.

That would have been too dark to land without the use of runway lights, at which time he could have simply made a decision to either return to Moorabbin or, when on approach to King Island, simply ask Melbourne to request that the duty officer attend to activate the landing lights. Not an unreasonable request.

The town of Currie was nearby and FOI records from that night indicate that Brian Jones had taken just 20 minutes to respond to the request from Melbourne to turn the runway lights on as a precaution after an "alert phase" had been activated due to a missing aircraft. This was from the time of receiving the call to the time of "lights on".

Twenty minutes was an entirely acceptable response time, so in reality, Fred was carrying plenty of fuel to "hold" overhead while any request was being actioned, given that holding fuel is calculated at reduced engine power and fuel flow, thereby increasing Fred's endurance. So the decision to "hold" overhead would have been even less critical for him should he have chosen to do so.

Since Melbourne would not have been contactable by VHF radio while the aircraft was on the ground at King Island, there was a note on the flight plan to indicate that Fred had intended to cancel his SAR time (a nominated time that triggers an automatic search-and-rescue response when not cancelled) from the briefing office landline telephone. There was also a public telephone at the airstrip available for emergencies if required.

This was all standard and while the question of why Fred had not requested lights at King Island still hasn't been answered conclusively, it is a moot point in determining anything to do with his mental state or the reason for his disappearance.

Any suggestion that Fred hadn't requested lights for a landing at King Island because he had intended to either stage his own disappearance or to take his own life and so would not have needed them anyway is, quite frankly, absurd.

These days, lights at small and regional airports are commonly activated remotely by a landing pilot from the aircraft anytime after dark using a discrete VHF radio frequency and are referred to as Pilot Activated Lighting or PAL. A very appropriate acronym on a bad night.

"LX" was marked on the flight plan, indicating that a survival beacon was fitted to the aircraft, but according to my enquiries, there was no such beacon fitted. The responsible person where the aircraft had been online for hire was adamant about that.

My observation was that both "Survival Beacon" (LX) and "Pilot Status" (L1) appear to be in another marker other than blue biro which Fred had used on the flight plan, but this is just a superficial observation and of no further relevance at this point.

Other than that, there is nothing untoward regarding the flight plan.

10

Spatial disorientation

Last light over The Otways

The term Spatial Disorientation describes a state of confusion that occurs in humans who are unable to effectively use visual input to distinguish which way is up and which way is down.

Maintaining balance is something we unknowingly do and it relies upon a complex interaction between our visual and sensory systems. Thankfully in everyday life, we aren't called upon to prove our competency in this way as if our life depended on it. But that is an instrument of a pilot's everyday working environment, and flying an aircraft in poor visibility is part of the job description.

How long someone can remain standing on one foot, firstly with eyes open and then with eyes closed, is a good example of the way humans are inherently unstable without visual input.

When an aircraft enters cloud, a pilot relies solely upon instruments and without them, it is commonly accepted in aviation medicine that, at the very best, he or she will last a maximum of two minutes before entering a life-threatening unstable flight attitude. From personal experience, maintaining control for two minutes without reference to instruments would be an Olympic-grade effort. In reality, it would be considerably less.

There are many recorded instances of spatial disorientation occurring in everything from light aircraft to large passenger jets, and if it is left to develop unchecked, the results can be fatal with the aircraft impacting the ground or water out of control and at high speed.

The privileges of a Class 4 Night Rating, which Fred held, allow for flight in VMC (Visual Meteorological Conditions), meaning on a clear night.

Naturally, this can sometimes be a challenging environment and pilots who hold that rating are trained to a basic level in the art of full instrument flight conditions should they need it.

Pilots are just as susceptible to spatial disorientation as anyone else during phases of flight where visibility is limited. But this was unlikely to be the case for Fred given the excellent conditions that prevailed that evening.

Acknowledging that flight without visual reference is a totally unnatural environment for the human sensory system, pilots can develop no inherent ability to avoid this state occurring when in conditions of impaired visibility.

While it is a nightmare scenario, I am certain that was not what happened to Fred, and I found it curious as to why the investigators should have left this option on the table as a likely scenario at all.

Many evenings I have sat on the headland at Apollo Bay in conditions identical to the ones described by the meteorological forecast on the 21st of October 1978, as well as those "actual" conditions as described in the witness statements of other pilots who had attended during the subsequent search phase that evening.

Quoting from the Air Safety Incident Report: "The first King Island search aircraft reported seeing the Cape Otway light when still well south of Cape Whickham, at 3,000 ft, a visibility of about 60 nautical miles." Cape Wickham is at the northern end of King Island.

This quote is used as a practical demonstration of the conditions that prevailed and to gauge the degree of difficulty Fred may have encountered in maintaining straight and level flight that evening.

The weather on the night was close to what one would call a bluebird evening, with light mid-level cloud.

Under such conditions, in the period between twelve minutes and six minutes prior to last light, the outline of the Cape Otway headland and the distant horizon are still quite distinguishable, practically enabling straight and level flight without reference to an aircraft's instrument panel.

There should have been nothing challenging about these conditions to a licensed pilot holding a Class 4 Instrument Rating in a completely serviceable aircraft equipped with an operational artificial horizon as a primary reference, as Fred's aircraft had.

The notion that Fred could clearly and calmly report the other craft's position relative to himself, its speed and the directions from which it was approaching while suffering the effects of spatial disorientation and possibly flying inverted for over six minutes is, at the very least, creative.

As already mentioned, according to aviation medicine, it is an accepted fact that a pilot can last for a maximum of only two minutes without visual references before succumbing to the effects of spatial disorientation, that being entering an unusual attitude such as a stall, spin, inverted flight or spiral dive.

On a number of occasions, I have had the privilege of listening to the original six-minute flight service conversation between Frederick Valentich and the Flight Service Duty Officer Steve Robey.

It is easy to positively certify the genuineness of that sound recording by the unmistakable, dulcet tone of Robey's voice, and this level of stress is not apparent to me at all when listening to Fred's voice in that original flight service recording.

I personally hold a firm opinion as to the capability of the pilot in command during the course of that whole six-minute period and that he was exercising full control of his aircraft at all times.

Moreover, it would appear to me that the investigators almost went out of their way to concoct the various possibilities to describe the final minutes of Frederick Valentich's flight.

For example, a statement lodged and submitted in the investigators' archival file notes is from a person who stated that while flying as "a passenger" in VH-DSJ a couple of months prior, an oil leak in the governor had resulted in an oil "film" (more likely it would be a line) on the windscreen of the aircraft "which could have led to strange visual effects when the sun was shining upon it", alluding to the possibility of spatial disorientation occurring. And this had made it into the official file report notes!

The likelihood of an oil leak being responsible for an illusion that somehow led to spatial disorientation in the pilot is even more implausible to me than the possibility of the aeroplane being intercepted by a UFO!

Not a lot of thought has been used in this scenario, as also twelve minutes before official last light, the sun would have well and truly set. And if the sun was up, there would have been virtually no chance at all of spatial disorientation occurring in the first place, given the conditions that prevailed.

It is preposterous to suggest that this was the possible cause for an accident and they, the authority, need to get their story straight. Was the sun out or not?

Notably, Fred was also tracking southeast at that point, away from the direction in which the sun would have set.

There seems to have been no critical analysis by the investigators of any of these scenarios, with press reports of the day often defaulting to a more sensational description of events.

In a prominent regional newspaper, there was a reference to a quote from a local Apollo Bay fisherman citing the green marine navigation lights on the hillside at Skenes Creek, five kilometres east of Apollo Bay, as being the likely source of the illusion for Fred that night: "… I reckon he was looking at that light and became confused."

This was obviously a dramatic reconstruction of events, but it was typical of the poetic licence employed by some of the media. No offence to the fisherman, but more likely a reflection of the substandard quality of reporting and research by the news-sheets of the day.

The very notion that Fred had been flying inverted and was looking at his own lights reflected on the surface of the water is an implausible, amateurish proposition at best even though it is probably the most commonly aired theory.

If anyone had reasonably workshopped the possibility of Fred flying inverted and being confused by his own aircraft's lights reflecting upon the surface of the ocean, it would have been plainly obvious that had this occurred, he would have been too low to maintain VHF radio communication with Melbourne, which requires "line of sight" to operate.

He couldn't have done both, flying that low in that region and maintaining clear and uninterrupted VHF radio communication with Melbourne Flight Service. It was impossible then and it is impossible now.

The 1968 Cessna 182L that Fred was flying that night also had a basic carburettor fuel system that was gravity-fed from the tanks in the wings above the fuselage. It is extremely reliable in normal phases of flight but unable to maintain power due to fuel starvation when inverted.

How long it would maintain power when inverted is a matter of conjecture, as inverted flight is an illegal manoeuvre in an aircraft such as the Cessna 182, but from those who should know, the response has been "not long". Maybe even just seconds.

In circumstances such as these, the power settings would not be, could not be, 23 inches manifold pressure and 2,400 RPM as Fred had clearly and calmly related over the radio, "23/24". (Refers to a cruise power setting of 76% bhp in that aeroplane).

More likely, under conditions of inverted flight where the engine had failed, the manifold pressure would read higher and be determined by the local ambient pressure QNH at that time, say 28", and the RPM would be considerably lower or zero as determined by whether the propeller was windmilling or not.

There is one other thing to add when it comes to the notion of a pilot losing control of his aircraft: excessive speed and the likelihood of disintegration of the aircraft when it impacts the surface of the ocean is highly probable. No doubt this would result in some wreckage eventually being found, not to mention the telltale slick that 270 litres of aviation gasoline would have left on the surface of the water.

But to date, 47 years later, there has been no sign of any of this.

11

Pending legal action

I have chosen to give this topic its own chapter rather than include it as part of the previous chapter.

It is to do with Fred illegally flying into cloud on two separate occasions without the proper qualification required, that being a current Instrument Rating and as a result, charges were apparently pending.

The DoT inquiry into Fred's disappearance made specific mention of this.

This allegation of pilot misbehaviour, justified or not, has for whatever reason been integrated with the report notes on that of the missing pilot, and the reason for doing so is again quite baffling.

I felt I had no choice but to give this matter its own chapter to point out not only the unfairness and irrelevance of it to the young pilot's disappearance, but also to headline the fact that it obviously reveals a qualification that Fred had gained by default.

He had gained experience in the demanding environment of full instrument flight conditions on at least two occasions, and perhaps more given what we know of human nature.

It means he would have been all too aware of the perils of spatial disorientation and the need to maintain a proper instrument scan to prevent the condition from occurring.

He would have not only been thoroughly cognisant of the importance of his artificial horizon as a primary reference instrument but also of the mental discipline required to control the aircraft and maintain level flight under those flight conditions.

Had he actually entered any conditions of limited visibility, these experiences could only have helped him, although I'm sure he hadn't as I have already explained.

While it is now impossible to be fully aware of the circumstances surrounding these breaches of air safety, the events must have been serious enough and significant enough for someone to have gone to all the trouble of filing the two separate incident reports.

It must go some way towards derailing their own (DoT's) argument that Fred had suffered from spatial disorientation that evening, even if it were possible due to poor visibility.

A common trait among pilots, young pilots in particular, is that they like to test their limits. Goes with the territory, much to the chagrin of the governing authorities.

Young Fred was no different.

12

Restricted airspace penetration

A "full reporting" flight plan meant that estimates for an aircraft's ETA at a particular waypoint or destination are nominated separately on the flight plan, and in those pre-GPS, pre-screen days, navigating was by a pencil line on a chart. In the close confines of controlled airspace, transiting VFR light aircraft lanes adjacent to a major city such as Sydney presented a high-workload environment, especially for a low-hour pilot who was unfamiliar with the route where turning points could be frequent.

It was a requirement that each ETA had to be within 2 minutes of a sector's completion, or a pilot was required to amend that arrival time en route.

This would have been the same for Fred when he flew a high-performance single-engine Cessna 210, VH-SRJ, from Melbourne's Moorabbin Airport up to Newcastle, New South Wales, with his then-girlfriend Rhonda as a passenger. Coincidentally, I have VH-SRJ in my logbook as well.

Any Restricted Area or Control Zone requires an airways clearance prior to entering, and aircraft that stray into those areas without such a clearance are deemed to have "penetrated" the zone and face scrutiny, possibly followed by corrective disciplinary action.

While transiting Sydney control zone on that flight, there was an unintended "penetration" of Sydney controlled airspace. While I am unaware of the details, I intend to briefly describe pilot workload and the unreasonableness in citing this incident as having any relevance in a missing person's investigation.

Calculating groundspeed was done by obtaining a positive fix with a feature on the ground and relating it back to the aviation World Aeronautical Chart (WAC) or Visual Terminal Chart (VTC) attached to a clipboard or spread across the knees of the pilot.

These charts are large and unwieldy, especially if they need to be completely unfolded.

That was called air-to-ground visual navigation (reading map to ground) and it relied on the weather being fair to reasonable. It also obviously relied on a pilot flying below and not above the cloud layer.

Flying and navigating solely by instruments in cloud is classed as flight under Instrument Flight Rules (IFR).

If the weather was poor and visibility was low, or when flying over the top of a cloud layer, the visual reference worked in reverse, ground-to-air, meaning a ground feature was first identified through a hole in the cloud layer and then related back to a feature on the chart.

For instance, identification from the air of a pair of wheat silos, a large power line, a rail junction or a coastal town seen through the hole in the cloud are all examples of positive visual fixes.

Groundspeed takes into account the effect of any wind and is gained from the time and distance between fixes.

Prior to GPS and screens, as was the case in those days, a pilot flying over the top of cloud had to hold his or her nerve and not alter heading without reason.

Often, this meant continuing under "dead reckoning" rules, taking into account the effects of wind prior to coming within range of a ground-based navigation aid or transiting out from over the top of a cloud layer.

On the flight to Newcastle, Fred had transited overhead a layer of cloud and that says something to me of this young pilot's confidence and ability.

Flight Service would mercilessly nag you about things like inaccurate estimates or tracking accuracy. They were the voice of authority you hated to hear burst over the radio, demanding a logical answer when things didn't sound right or numbers didn't add up at their end.

This requirement to micromanage flights and report progress generally isn't mandatory today, and all that is required is that a nominated "responsible person" on the ground can hold details for a pilot's final estimated time of arrival at the destination.

VFR pilots are largely left alone when outside of control areas, thus removing the burden of having Big Brother watching over your shoulder. It is more practical and a big stress reliever.

Charts are optional too for a private pilot and although there is a legal minimum tablet screen size to be used in the cockpit, some pilots fly on their smartphone and they can navigate quite successfully this way, even around the narrow confines of controlled airspace lanes while leaving the tablet in the briefcase with the charts.

As there were no electronics in the aircraft in those days, estimates were calculated on a Round Flight Computer which was nothing more than a round slide rule that pilots affectionately call a "prayer wheel". It does not incorporate buttons, screens or electronic readouts.

That was very much the simplified version of the world that Fred and I were entering at about the same time. If you weren't happy to push yourself and if you didn't like a challenge or adrenaline rush, then the life of a commercial pilot wasn't for you.

It's obvious to me that Fred did, and he was happy to push himself and push the limits as any good aspiring young pilot would do. By their very nature, pilots aren't retiring wallflowers.

The environment for flying is far more practical these days than it was in Fred's day. Today, a pilot is generally only required to navigate with charts during their initial flight test. Back then, the pressure of not having the option of technology and the reality of having to navigate by chart full-time, all day, every day, was by and large a VFR pilot's lot, especially in remote Outback Australia.

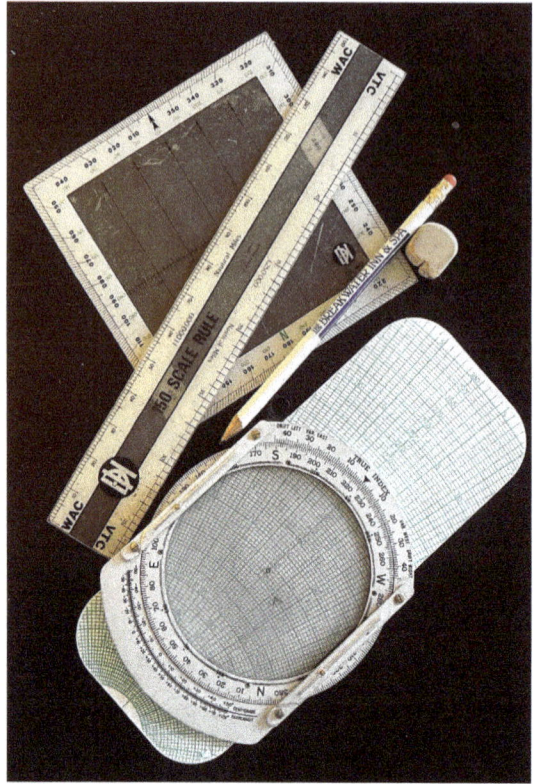

In those pre-screen days, we navigated by pencil line on a chart

A fast single-engine aircraft such as a Cessna 210 like the VH-SRJ can be moving across the ground at close to 300 kilometres per hour (5 kilometres per minute) and obviously faster with any tailwind component.

At that speed and in that pre-screen era, when having to rely solely upon attaining visual fixes and navigating only by a pencil line on a chart, things happen very quickly.

A turbulent hot northerly wind would make it just that more difficult.

While returning from Newcastle in VH-SRJ, Fred had penetrated a restricted area, and this somehow made it into the investigators' file notes. What it had to do with a missing pilot isn't at all apparent to me.

Many others I know had also made unplanned airspace penetrations. I know I had.

Given the clear and unambiguous flight path afforded by screen technology while transiting Control Areas (CTA), these incidents today, thankfully, aren't anywhere near as common.

To obtain a flying licence takes commitment and persistence in getting it right. After researching all I could about Fred, I believe that he had the ability to get it right and, like any of us who were human, he also had the ability to get it wrong.

Flying is like that; it tests you and often finds your weaknesses. In that respect and from all I can determine, Fred was like any other pilot I have known.

I asked Ross about Fred regarding the hire of the high-performance Cessna 210 from SAS to fly up to Newcastle. He replied that Fred was a good pilot and that SAS would have thoroughly checked him out in that aircraft and confirmed his competency prior to signing him out.

In my opinion, Fred must have been at least average or above average as a pilot to have flown that particular aircraft on a VFR flight plan up to Newcastle and back with barely 150 hours of flight time logged.

It's impossible to give his actual logged flight hours at the time of his last flight because his logbook was never found. I would have to assume it was in his flight bag in the aircraft with him when he flew down to King Island on the day of his disappearance.

The Shipwreck Coast

Part of the enjoyment of my work day was the people I met. With Terry Branstead

View from the airport street, looking north across Marengo Bay

The role of "single pilot" was a high workload environment especially back in those days, significantly higher than it is today. In the past, I have expressed this to young pilots in my employ and watched their eyes glaze over. I had learnt to recognise when the shutters went up.

Looking back, the aloneness of that workplace suited me and I miss that now.

As a sidenote, on one trip following a road out west to Kingston in South Australia to pick up a load of crayfish and very much under the stress of weather, I was reading "ground to map" because when flying at a low altitude in not-so-brilliant visibility, things can happen very fast. By default, the "ground to map" method of navigation takes over.

I remember being relieved to positively identify a small town in a valley out west as Harrow on the Glenelg River, a place I would come to know well as the nearest local town to my small farm at Tarrayoukyan to the south, in the Western District of Victoria.

Western Victoria is notorious for low cloud and bad weather, and those experiences stood me in good stead for the years that followed flying in and out of Apollo Bay.

I often have cause to reflect on these and other geographical coincidences that have occurred at various times in my flying career.

Was it merely happenstance or was it fate that had caused me to research and become so involved with the disappearance of a young pilot called Frederick Valentich?

I prefer to think it was fate.

13

A handwritten letter

Scrolling through the pages and pages of documents uncovered by FOI revealed much information. (Credit to Mr Keith Basterfield for his persistence in extracting the cache, released in 2012.) A lot of it was in duplicate, not completely apparent until you got your teeth into reading it.

Either way, there was enough to scrutinise and cross-check, with a large number of the documents being almost illegible handwritten reports that took time to decipher and evaluate.

It goes with the era, well before keypads, computers and connectivity, adding considerably to the opportunity for me to be creative and descriptive with the story along the way. Not that truth can ever be compromised, but more born out of a reverence and a longing for the way life was back then.

Not so long ago, life was simpler and people of my generation who were there miss that.

Harder but simpler.

Funny, just yesterday I saw a Facebook post about living in the 1970s and someone had captioned the photo of a group of teenagers in their bathers, standing in front of an old Holden sedan with a surfboard strapped to the roof rack:

> *I want to go back to the seventies and live there forever.*

Says it all.

As I read through the files, some handwritten documents were placed in the "too hard" basket and went to the end of the line before I had the energy to tackle them. Actually, some went to the end of the line a few times before I got to look at them.

Clive's handwritten letter was included in the Valentich file and was one of those that I passed over a couple of times.

I chose to pass it by probably because it was too arranged, too neat. His well-ordered straight lines seemed to use up every square millimetre on the page. Who writes like that? Looked a bit like ants with ink on their feet had been walking across the paper, and I assumed that a letter like that was going to be somewhat matter-of-fact and boring, being the reason I hadn't bothered to read it in the first round.

What I had mistaken as ordinary in the language of Clive's letter turned out instead to be something more revealing. It was that of the writer having an analytical mind, and in the subject matter of his ordered ant tracks was evidence of a person who was also a visionary and a critical thinker.

His views were offered honestly and without the benefit of "spellcheck". It reads simply and without pretence.

It appealed to the interpretive mind in the same way as perhaps a genuine indigenous artwork does or a piece of unique Australian "depression furniture", without the beholder ever being aware of the disarming simplicity subconsciously imbued within it as being the reason that they are so attracted to that work in the first place.

That's the category in which I place Clive's letter.

While its content has only a little direct connection with the Valentich case, it has its own disarming simplicity, being a light-hearted and uncomplicated characterisation of regional UFO sightings and encounters of the day in the eastern part of Victoria.

Seeking permission to publish, I had finally tracked him down, and I might add that he wasn't at all easy to find. Google didn't have a clue, and I was about to find out why.

This was because of the way he had covered his tracks over the years, by laying low, staying at precisely the same address as was handwritten in the top corner of his letter 47 years earlier, and by not succumbing at all to the expectations of the modern e-world.

Cunning. Who would have suspected it?

Like an old Wollemi Pine in an undiscovered valley, he didn't just seem to be at peace; he was flourishing.

In a welcome landline telephone conversation with him, I learned that nothing had altered in Clive's life except his age. At eighty years young, he had refused to be swayed by the expectations of the modern world by not owning a computer or having an email address, nor even owning a mobile phone.

He also spoke to me about his plans of having some time off soon, so he could enjoy what was left of his life.

He was quick to add that he hadn't had to advertise in his small business since 1987 and that he had kept going through the use of the telephone, the regular mail network and, of course, by word of mouth.

The suspicious side of me was in overdrive at this point. I hadn't expected the double left hooks of simplicity and honesty that Clive had obviously chosen as the standards by which he had lived his life, and I was having trouble processing it.

It isn't difficult for me to think of Clive Downie as East Gippsland's answer to Cliff Young, the enigmatic 61-year-old 1983 ultramarathon winner and potato farmer from Colac, Victoria.

From the outset, he impressed me as a person who would find it impossible to tell a lie, and so the honest testimony of his letter is an important time capsule written in a pre-internet, pre-connectivity era.

Those same qualities are evident in this disarmingly descriptive letter to Fred's father, Guido Valentich, dated 29th of October 1978, penned just eight days after his son Fred's disappearance.

This missive begins with clarity and a sympathetic openness for Guido's loss that leads the reader into the archive of Clive's perspective on life, past, present and future.

Its lighthearted message is both as innocent as it is relevant, embodying a certain honesty, that being the honesty of an open mind.

The letter is a piece of Australiana, thankfully held on file in the National Archive of Australia where it duly belongs, and it is also an unfortunate fact of life that we cannot place Clive in the National Archive with it as well, for as far as I can determine, he too is a true-blue National Treasure.

Clive's handwritten letter is disarmingly simple and so is his ability to evaluate mankind's location in the universal timescale when he made the statement in 1978: "Imagine 100 years ago someone talking about taking a picture, converting it to a radio signal, sending it at the speed of light and reconstructing it into the visible mode again in the TV set. The man who talked about that 100 years ago would have been ridiculed."

Other observations written in his letter of 1978 described the futuristic possibility of teleportation also being a matter-of-fact invention of the future, indicating an openness and acceptance to what could and most probably will be in store for humankind, commenting also, "… imagine how smart we will be when we can reverse gravity …"

A visionary statement in 1978.

What is also embedded in the script, and highly significant to me in the context of this case, are the multiple references to witness accounts of the effect that UFOs have when in close proximity to the ignition systems of internal combustion engines: being that they cease to operate. This is a common characteristic.

> *Since then I have spoken to many people some had ignition failure with Gasoline engines when a light hovered above + buzzed them. The sweat ran down their necks and their foot hard down on the accelerator did nothing.*

The accounts in his letter are particularly relevant when considering the effect that the other craft reportedly had on Fred's aircraft's engine performance, as evidenced in his own words to Melbourne Flight Service in his last radio transmission.

"Delta Sierra Juliet the engine is rough idling. I've got it set at 23/24 and the thing is coughing."

How is it that observations of UFOs and their various behavioural characteristics are so similar around the world as they were for Fred prior to the advent of the internet and social media?

There is an easy and obvious explanation: they are true.

Below is a scan of Clive's letter to Fred's father, Mr Guido Valentich.

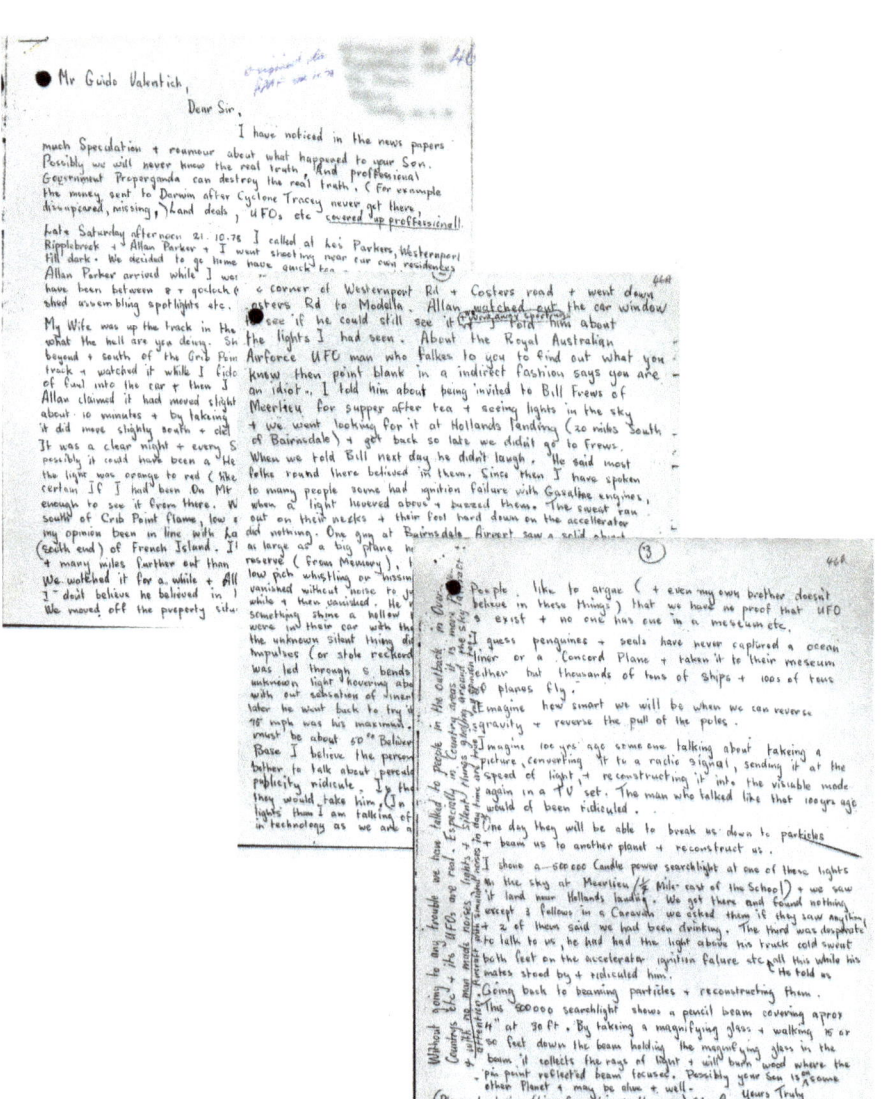

Below is Clive's letter reproduced verbatim.

Mr Guido Valentich,

Dear Sir,

I have noticed in the newspapers much speculation + rumour about what happened to your Son. Possibly we will never know the real truth, And professional Government Propergandah can destroy the real truth. (For example the money sent to Darwin after Cyclone Tracy never got there, disappeared, missing,) Land deals, UFOs etc <u>covered up professional.</u>

Late Saturday afternoon 21.10.78 I called at Les Parkers, Westernport Ripplebrook + Allan Parker + I went shooting near our own residences till dark. We decided to go home have quick tea + go spotlighting. Allan Parker arrived while I was eating my tea + go out spotlighting. Alan Parker arrived while I was eating my tea + I reckon it must have been between 8 + 9 o'clock (PM) 21.10.78 that I was down our shed assembling spotlights etc.

My wife was up the track in the headlights + we yelled out to her what the hell are you doing. She had a bright light in the sky beyond + south of the Crib Point Gas flame. Allan went on up the track + watched it while I fiddled about + pumped 10 or 12 gallons of fuel into the car + then I drove up the track for a look. Allan claimed it had moved slightly so I guess I watched it for about 10 minutes + by taking a bareing on lights on the ground it did move slightly south + did loose altitude again very slowly. It was a clear night + every Star could be seen if it was not a star possibly it could have ben a Helicopter Hovering at great distance the light was orange to red (like a distant car tail light) + I am certain if I had ben on Mt Baw Baw it would have been bright enough to see it from there. We only saw a light. It was south of Crib Point flame, low over the horizon + would of in my opinion been in line with Lang Lang Jetty or the bottom end (south end) of French Island. It appeared to bee well out over the sea + and many miles further out than land.

We watched it for a while + Allan was impressed as until then I don't believe he believed in lights in the sky etc We moved off the property situated 6 miles south of Drouin on the corner of Westernport Rd + Costers road + went down Costers Rd to Modella. Allan watched out the car window to see if he could still see it + we went away shooting + I told him the lights I had seen. About the Royal Australian Airforce man who talks to you to find out what you know then point blank in a indirect fashion says you are an idiot. I told him about being invited to Bill Frews of Meerlieu for supper after tea + seeing lights in the sky + we went looking for it at Hollands landing (20 miles south of Bairnsdale) + got back so late we didn't go to Frews. When we told Bill next day he didn't laugh. He said most folks around believed in them. Since then I have spoken to many people some **had ignition failure with Gasoline engines** *when a light hovered above + buzzed them. The sweat ran down their necks and their foot hard down on the accelerator did nothing. One guy at Bairnsdale airport saw a solid object as large as a big plane hovering above a (football ground) or local reserve (from Memory). He told me it had no wings made a slight low pitch whistling or hissing noise + when it started to move it vanished without a noise to just a speck in the sky. It hovered there a while +* **then vanished**. *He knew of people who had a noiseless something shine a hollow beam searchlight down on them while they were in their car with* **the ignition dead** *+ these people feel that the unknown silent thing did a computer read out on their brain impulses (or stole reckords from their memory). Another guy was led through the S bends at up to 115 mph in his car by an unknown light hovering above the car. The s bends were done without sensation or inertia (or Syntrifugal forse) + latter, days later he went back to try it all over again in the same car 75 mph was his maximum. People here in Ripplebrook their must be about 50% Believers. At meerlieu not far from the RAAF Base I believe the percentage may be higher. Not many people bother to talk about peculiar things that they have seen because of publicity ridicule. In the case of your Son if they wanted him they would take him. (In my opinion) + I have seen more of these lights than I am talking of here, whoever controls them is as advanced in technology as we are advanced over a dog.*

People like to argue (+ even my own brother doesn't believe in these things) that we have no proof that a UFOs exist + no one has one in a museum etc.

I guess penguins + seals have never captured an ocean liner or a Concord Plane + taken it to their museum either but thousands of tons of ships + 100s of tons of planes fly.

Imagine how smart we will be when we can reverse gravity + reverse the pull of the poles.

Imagine 100 yrs ago someone talking about taking a picture, converting it to a radio signal, sending it at the speed of light + reconstructing it into the visible mode again in a TV set. The man who talked about that 100 years ago would of been ridiculed.

One day they will be able to break us down into particles + beam us to another planet + reconstruct us.

I shone 500 000 Candle power searchlight at one of these lights in the sky at Meerlieu (1/4 Mile east of the School) + we saw it land near Hollands landing. We got there and found nothing except 3 fellows in a Caravan we asked if they had seen anything + 2 of them said we had been drinking. The third was desperate to talk to us, he had had the lights above his truck cold sweat both feet on the accelerator ignition failure etc He told us all this while his mates stood by and ridiculed him.

Going back to beaming particles + reconstructing them. This 5000 000 searchlight shows a pencil beam covering approx 4" at 30 ft. By taking a magnifying glass + walking 15 or 80 feet down the beam holding the magnifying glass in the beam it collects the rays of light + will burn the wood where the pin point reflected beam focusses. Possibly your Son is on some other Planet + may be alive + well.

Yours Truly

Clive Downie

(Please do not give this information to the press.)

It has been said that "imagination" is more important than knowledge and that "intuition" is the highest form of intelligence because it derives an answer solely from inductive reasoning.

Clive's letter indicates a mind that embodies both of these qualities. It speaks plainly of what will be.

When considering just how far mankind has progressed in the few short years since the day Clive penned his letter, our growth in knowledge has been and can increasingly be described as "exponential". Yesterday's science fiction is today's reality.

To better grasp the enormity of the concept of an exponential growth in knowledge, consider that by placing a grain of rice on the first square of a chessboard and then doubling that amount on each successive square, by the sixty-fourth square, the amount of rice will equal 18.4 quintillion grains, many times the total of the world's annual rice production. Enough to cover Manhattan Island with a pile of rice seven kilometres high!

Or that after doubling and redoubling a piece of paper fifty times, how thick will the stack eventually be? One hundred and forty-nine million kilometres, or from here to the sun thick!

Consider also that in 2022 the James Webb telescope positioned a million miles from earth, utilizing deep field image technology and focusing on a "blank" patch of sky no bigger than the size of a grain of sand held at arms length, had discovered thousands of unknown galaxies billions of light years from earth.

Given what we know of UFO sightings both here and overseas, and given what we know of the vastness of never-ending space, it would seem arrogant to discount the prospect of ever encountering another non-human life form, a life form that is perhaps a thousand or even a million years ahead of us, exponentially more advanced in terms of its own knowledge and development.

It is important to bear all this in mind when deciding whether or not Frederick Valentich could have just been calling it as he saw it, one perfect evening off the coast of Cape Otway in October 1978.

14

The Cape Otway Lighthouse log

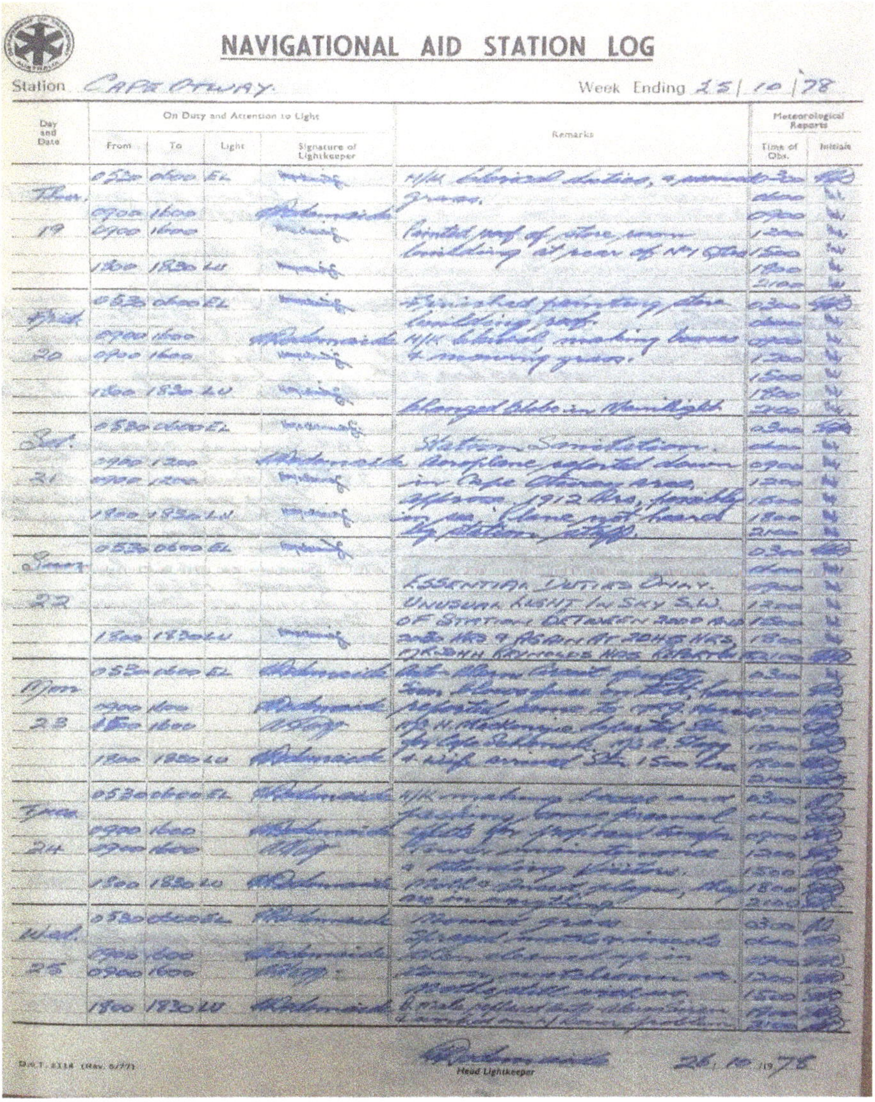

NAA: A14074, 20 - Cape Otway navigational station log book[LH-4], 1977 – 1978.

The copy of the handwritten log from the Cape Otway Lighthouse reflects a moment frozen in time.

It is a genuine eyewitness testimony written in the Cape Otway Lighthouse keeper's log by a professional observer.

The log states that on the evening of Fred's disappearance, being October 21st, "Plane not heard by station staff."

Fred's flight plan noted that his track down the coast from Moorabbin Airport was 225 degrees magnetic and that at Cape Otway, he would take up a track of 155 degrees magnetic direct to King Island, a heading change of 70 degrees left, being to the south southwest. Almost a right angle.

Cape Otway Lighthouse

So, it made sense to "cut the corner" at this point and it was common practice among transiting VFR pilots. It would explain why the staff at the Cape Otway Lighthouse hadn't heard the aircraft pass by that evening, either going out or coming back.

Fred had made at least three prior trips to King Island and so would have been fully aware of the benefits of gaining some time by "cutting the corner".

From experience when navigating solely by the use of charts the tendency was to always make a position report for "Cape Otway" early and more to the north east of that location.

Call it impatience or call it a trick of the eye, that was a common occurrence and not completely evident to me until I started to use screens as a primary navigation guide.

This then would have placed Fred east of his original flight planned track to King Island and closer to Apollo Bay at his point of diversion by at least 2 nautical miles but maybe much more. This is in support of a practical timeline for him having been able to make it back in time to Apollo Bay circuit area where he was seen by Merv right on last light. He would also have been completely aware of the existence of the little coastal grass Authorised Landing Area (ALA) marked on the aviation navigation "WAC chart" located in the valley amongst the coastal scrub, at Marengo just south of Apollo Bay. From my recollection the coastal scrub encroached and it was far less distinct than it is today.

As a pilot, he would have made a mental note of its location. It was an "alternate" and so in any sort of emergency, it would have given him options.

On October 22nd, the day after Fred disappeared, the lighthouse log also clearly recorded in capital letters, "Unusual Light in the sky S.W. of station Between 2000 and 2030 Hrs and again at 2045 Hrs."

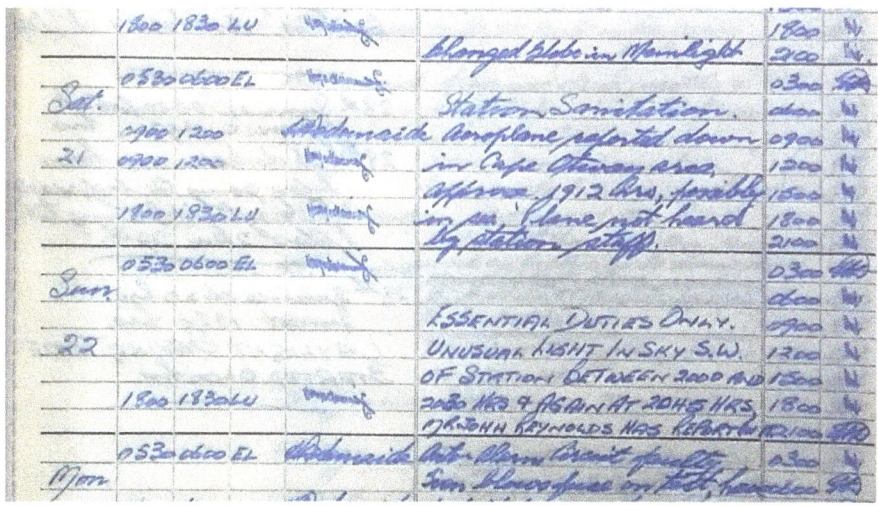

An observation from a professional observer should carry some weight, but again, it is apparent that no members of the DoT investigating team either asked about the possibility of a transiting aircraft or of anything unusual that might have taken place on that night or subsequent nights.

Surely, this would have been another crucial point of inquiry for any balanced investigation attempting to solve the riddle of the disappearance of the lone airman, whose last position report to Melbourne Flight Service was in fact that very location, Cape Otway.

I concede that while I can only be as thorough as I can possibly be, I cannot be certain that the lightstation was never contacted.

Nothing that I had found relating to a strange light having been observed by the lighthouse keeper was ever revealed as connected with the disappearance of pilot Frederick Valentich in the DoT's file notes, held in the vaults of the National Archives.

The sighting of a strange light would have been an inconvenient truth for the investigators, but surely, under the circumstances, it should have been highly noteworthy.

What I am certain about is that if they had contacted the lightstation, then there was no record of it contained in the FOI files that I had seen. And if they had gained access to the lighthouse keeper's log, then that information was never made public.

If that was the case, then it was concealment of relevant information regarding an investigation of a missing person, and as such, was far worse than what would otherwise be regarded as simply malpractice, or even incompetence for not ever having attended.

15

The DoT Accident & Incident Report

The DoT Accident and Incident Report contains an accurate transcription of the final six-minute radio conversation between Frederick Valentich and Melbourne Flight Service operator Steve Robey.

It is prefaced with a short description of the relevant events and ends with "Opinion As to Cause":

The reason for the disappearance of the aircraft has not been determined.

Note the absence of the acronym "UFO" in any of the recorded narrative which in this case, is an unexpected omission for someone preparing a famous death and dramatic exit by suicide.

Image courtesy of the National Archives of Australia. NAA: B1497, V116/783/1047.

Extract from the Department Of Transport Aircraft Accident Investigation Summary Report.

The pilot reported Cape Otway at 1900 hours and the next transmission received from the aircraft was at 1906:14 hours. The following communications between the aircraft and Melbourne Flight Service Unit were recorded from this time onwards.

TIME	FROM	TEXT
1906:14	VH-DSJ	Melbourne this is Delta Sierra Juliet, is there any known traffic below five thousand?
:23	FSU	Delta Sierra Juliet, no known traffic.
:26	VH-DSJ	Delta Sierra Juliet, I am, seems to be a large aircraft below five thousand.
:46	FSU	Delta Sierra Juliet what type of aircraft is it?
:50	VH-DSJ	Delta Sierra Juliet, I cannot affirm. It is four bright, it seems to me like landing lights.
1907:04	FSU	Delta Sierra Juliet
:32	VH-DSJ	Melbourne this is Delta Sierra Juliet the aircraft has just passed over me at least a thousand feet above.
:43	FSU	Delta Sierra Juliet roger, and it is a large aircraft, confirm?
:47	VH-DSJ	Ah, unknown due to the speed it's travelling. Is there any Airforce aircraft in the vicinity?
:57	FSU	Delta Sierra Juliet, no known aircraft in the vicinity.
1908:18	VH-DSJ	Melbourne, it's approaching now from due east towards me.

TIME	FROM	TEXT
:28	FSU	Delta Sierra Juliet.
:42	VH-DSJ	// open mic for 2 seconds //
:49	VH-DSJ	Delta Sierra Juliet, it seems to me that he's playing some sort of game. He's flying over me two three times at a time, at speeds I could not identify.
1909:02	FSU	Delta Sierra Juliet roger, what is your actual level?
:06	VH-DSJ	My level is four and a half thousand. Four five zero zero.
:11	FSU	Delta Sierra Juliet, and confirm you cannot identify the aircraft?
:14	VH-DSJ	Affirmative.
:18	FSU	Delta Sierra Juliet, roger, standby.
:28	VH-DSJ	Melbourne, Delta Sierra Juliet, it's not an aircraft it is // open mic for 2 seconds //
:46	FSU	Delta Sierra Juliet, Melbourne, can you describe the aircraft?
1909:52	VH-DSJ	Delta Sierra Juliet, as it's flying past it's a long shape // open mic for 3 seconds // cannot identify more than that, it has such speed // open mic for 3 seconds // Before me right now Melbourne.
1910:07	FSU	Delta Sierra Juliet, roger and how large would the, er, object be?
:20	VH-DSJ	Delta Sierra Juliet, Melbourne, it seems like it's stationary. What I'm doing right now is orbiting and the thing is just orbiting on top of me also. It's got a green light and sort of metallic like. It's all shiny on the outside.

TIME	FROM	TEXT
:43	FSU	Delta Sierra Juliet.
:48	VH-DSJ	Delta Sierra Juliet // open mic for 5 seconds // It's just vanished.
:57	FSU	Delta Sierra Juliet.
1911:03	VH-DSJ	Melbourne, would you know what kind of aircraft I've got? Is it a type of military aircraft?
:08	FSU	Delta Sierra Juliet, confirm the er, aircraft just vanished?
:14	VH-DSJ	Say again.
:17	FSU	Delt Sierra Julette, is the aircraft still with you?
:23	VH-DSJ	Delta Sierra Juliet, aah nor // open mic 2 seconds // it's now, approaching from the southwest.
:37	FSU	Delta Sierra Juliet.
:52	VH-DSJ	Delta Sierra Juliet, the engine is, is rough idling. I've got it set at twenty three, twenty four and the thing is coughing.
1912:04	FSU	Delta Sierra Juliet, roger what are your intentions?
:09	DSJ	My intentions are ah to go to King Island ah Melbourne that strange aircraft is hovering on top of me again. // open mic for 2 seconds // It is hovering and it's not an aircraft.
:22	FSU	Delta Sierra Juliet.
:28	VH-DSJ	Delta Sierra Juliet, Melbourne, // 17 seconds of open mic //
:49	FSU	Delta Sierra Juliet, Melbourne…

16

Ross

I had never previously met Ross but we had had an extended phone conversation about seven years ago. We didn't know each other but Ross was very trusting and open to helping with any background information on Frederick Valentich.

We eventually met at his country property in eastern Victoria and immediately, I felt there was a natural connection, based not only on aviation but on agriculture, and so I had used up a lot of my timeslot that day on matters rural.

If the home property was any measure of the man, then Ross was certainly a heavyweight. A self-made man. Sprawling and expansive, it felt more like the set of a Netflix mini-series.

The only thing missing was the big brass belt buckle, I thought, as I approached him to shake his hand in the front courtyard.

Ross's aviation career began in Warrnambool in 1976, where he earned his wings and progressed to owning and operating one of the biggest flying schools in the southern hemisphere, starting off with one aircraft and finishing with 72 Cessna aircraft, 110 staff and 600 students.

He was also a member of the Aviation Safety Forum (ASF) which was set up to advise the Australian Civil Aviation Safety Authority (CASA) on legislative issues. This is recognition of his vision within the industry.

Ross's flight training school, BTech Aviation, pioneered university aviation studies at Melbourne's Swinburne University in 1990, adding a next-level opportunity and professionalism to an industry that needed it so badly.

Ironically, Fred would have benefited greatly from all of this if it were available in his day.

Ross retired from full-time aviation in 2008 but had kept his hand in flying Cessna 500 series citation business jets up until 2023.

Most importantly, he had worked as an instructor at Southern Air Services (SAS), where he gained his initial qualification in September 1978, two months prior to Fred's disappearance.

Both his testimony and his opinions are greatly valued.

Fred disappeared in a Cessna 182L, VH-Delta Sierra Juliet, which at the time was online for hire at SAS, Moorabbin.

Ross's opinion of Fred was broad and well-founded, based on their time spent together as students at commercial pilot ground school in the critical early months of 1978, and then later when Ross became an instructor at SAS where Fred was hiring aircraft and learning to fly.

An investigator's note quoted four SAS pilots and instructors who knew Fred.

Warren Dunlop: "Valentich was a sensible pilot."

Martin Dalton: "Quiet, sincere, sensible. Got on well with everyone. Never spoke of UFOs."

Ross: "Full of enthusiasm, never depressed. Got on well with people. Only had Commercial Meteorology to do."

Bob Hope (instructor): "Flew with Valentich on Tuesday afternoon to check him on type VH-DSJ C182. Saw him just prior to departure and he seemed perfectly sober and in a good frame of mind."

Ross's opinion was that Fred was energetic, affable, well-liked and regarded as a bit of a storyteller among his peers at Mansell's aviation ground school. He was full of life.

They began ground school together and would have ended together, but Fred fell behind in his ground school subjects due to a number of factors that I have already mentioned.

By Ross's own admission, Fred was probably better than himself at academia, but he had burned the candle at both ends by combining study and working full-time, including some nights, so that his full potential was never realised.

This is a valuable assessment of Fred's mental capability and goes a long way to challenge the inferences in the BASI report notes citing low IQ.

The aviation subjects at any level, Private, Commercial or Air Transport Pilots Licence (Airline Licence) are tertiary qualifications and are not to be taken lightly. These subjects command the full attention of any candidate, regardless of IQ. Certainly, attending ground school and going to work full-time and expecting to achieve passes in all those difficult subjects was and still is hopelessly unrealistic.

At the time, Fred was working as a storeman at an army disposal shop in Moonee Ponds and previously on nightshifts at the Astro Bar at Tullamarine Airport, sometimes arriving for class late as a result of having slept in.

Clearly, it was a study regime that was completely untenable.

Ross and I were in complete lockstep with that assessment, and it felt like old times as I revealed my own failures in these subjects and then having to re-sit. And Ross revealed a few too! We both laughed about that as we can now all these years later. But to see your friends gaining ground ahead of you, as Fred would have, must have been soul-destroying for him, a dedicated pilot at heart.

Perhaps the most revealing part was when Ross explained the circumstances following Fred's failure of his first flight test on his Restricted Private Pilot's licence. Ross wasn't completely sure, but he suspected it was something like not being up to speed with the "forced landing" (engine failure) part of the flight test. Again, easy to do, but the reaction from his father, Guido, was very revealing and not at all consistent with what I had come to know about him.

According to Ross's personal testimony, Guido went to the flight school and heavily berated the testing officer for failing his son.

Words were said to the effect that Fred was a very good pilot and didn't deserve to be failed. I am told it was a heated exchange.

By any account, it was a rare occurrence and something I have never witnessed or even heard of in all my 45 years of aviation. I wasn't involved in flight training, but it is exceptional behaviour whichever way you choose to look at it.

During an investigation such as this, there are watershed moments, and this was one of them for me.

This account reveals plenty about the pressure Fred might have been under because of the desire to please his father, and it most likely would have been highly embarrassing for him as well.

Fred was living at home and it would be fair to think that the home environment must have been stifling for him when factoring in his performance track record in ground school theory.

It would appear there may have been an element of control exercised by his father that wasn't so obvious at first glance. This, combined with the straitened financial circumstances that Fred found himself in, must have made the task of achieving his dream of becoming a commercial pilot at times seem almost impossible.

Something needed to change, but by all accounts, nothing did.

My last questions to Ross were big ones, and I'd been saving them.

"Was this at all reflecting on Fred's mental health and do you think that he was depressed about his situation?"

Ross answered, "Most definitely," but then added that he could have come to him or any other of the boys to talk about it, but regretfully, he never did.

So, then I asked point-blank whether Fred was capable of self-harm as a result of all this.

Ross replied, "Yes, I do."

Given all the previous discussion that had taken place about Fred's life and disposition, Ross's answer wasn't exactly a surprise, but it was an unwelcome reality check all the same.

It is also important to be clear that this was an opinion proffered a long time after the fact and somewhat at odds with his previous statement.

The opinions that may have transpired in the minds of all those young men in Fred's circle, including Ross, prior to that fateful flight aren't available for scrutiny, but I suspect that the response to that same question, had it been asked prior to that fateful day, would not have been so confronting.

By this, I mean that hindsight is a wonderful thing, and if the question on the subject of Fred's mental health had been asked prior to that last flight, then the answers may have been quite different.

Given that the prospect of suicide was well-aired after the fact, negative aspects can often become magnified in the minds of individuals over the years, and especially so after such a controversial and significant event such as this.

According to Ross, the weather was beyond poor on Wednesday, October 18th, when Fred had booked out the Cessna 182 VH-DSJ for a trip to King Island, so instead, he had spent a couple of hours at Southern Air Services talking about flying with Ross and one other staff member.

Ross had said they had quite a job to convince him not to do the flight that day, but Fred had said that he had an airline pilot and his two children to pick up at King Island. This remains unverified.

What is notable and important also, for reasons that will become obvious later, is that according to Ross, who was in attendance on the day, Fred had chosen to wear his Air Force uniform, being the Wednesday prior to his disappearance. Nothing wrong with that, but they had all found it a bit over the top. No reason why he had chosen to wear it that day has ever been established.

So, Fred had worn the uniform without apparent reason on the Wednesday prior. Was he wearing it again for his flight on the following Saturday? Establishing this is of major importance to this investigation.

Fred had recently sought to join the Air Force but had failed the entrance exam, which by all accounts is a demanding exam.

Over the years, I knew plenty of pilots who had been turned away from the RAAF as a result of failing the entrance exam, but again, the DoT had made particular note of this in Fred's file relating to his disappearance, highlighting it in a negative way, somehow insinuating that he was a low standard candidate and also that he had a low IQ.

In any event, on Wednesday, October 18th, Fred was wearing the Air Force Cadet uniform which consisted of a light blue shirt and navy pants, dark polished shoes and may have been wearing an Air Force blazer jacket as well.

Ross didn't see Fred on Saturday, October 21st, the day he disappeared, so he couldn't personally vouch for anything that occurred on that day, only what he was told.

All these years later, there were very few people that I have spoken to who saw Fred on the day of his departure, and none who are willing to positively recall what he had been wearing.

Conceivably, Fred could have simply worn a pullover if he had worn his uniform to work that morning at the Army Disposals. It has become important to establish just what Fred had been wearing when he departed Moorabbin Airport in DSJ later that day.

According to Rhonda, he probably would not have worn his uniform on that Saturday morning, but she couldn't be sure because she hadn't seen him that day. Was it possible that he was intending to wear it as a surprise for her for their evening together at Grandy's?

While I commit to truthfully relaying the facts as they are related to me and while I respect Ross's judgment, I don't believe that Fred did take his own life, and that suicide is still a long bow to draw.

Lastly, in a later discussion that I had with Ross, he admitted that despite statements having been subsequently taken from those working at SAS, and Ross cannot recall how and when they were taken, both he and the other pilots were stunned by the lack of activity from the investigators directly subsequent to Fred's disappearance.

No activity aside from a waiting room full of clairvoyants and psychics attempting to channel Fred, and who were subsequently given short shrift by the then Canadian owner, Mr Ken Novits.

In Ross's own words and I quote: "I think I felt empty as Fred was missing and there did not appear to be any great search going on for him as we do today. I flew down to the area around Cape Otway the next day at the same time looking for him or aircraft wreckage but of course saw nothing. There were no other aircraft looking for DSJ at this time which I thought was unusual. It would be interesting to know what search took place as we heard only that the RAAF had searched the area. It was surreal the lack of knowledge passed onto us of Fred's disappearance. It all seemed to be about UFO's in the press and that was it!!"

If there was to be a fair appreciation of what may have occurred that day, then logically, any reasonable line of inquiry should have started by visiting the establishment from where Fred had hired the aircraft and from where he was learning to fly. Garnering the final opinions of those friends and colleagues who knew him best and saw him last while everything was still fresh in their mind should have been paramount, especially in light of the controversial circumstances under which Fred had disappeared.

But this hadn't occurred.

No questions were asked.

No one ever came.

17

Rhonda Rushton

Rhonda and Fred

Rhonda Rushton was Fred's girlfriend, and he was her man. They were in love and had become engaged and had plans to marry.

My old notebook from 2018 contained one of the first attempts at putting pen to paper in the writing of this book, and it is apparent that my passion and focus on certain aspects have shifted dramatically throughout the course of time.

I chose not to disregard this small paragraph because it still has a relevance in some way in setting the scene for the relationship that existed between these two young people. It remains in the background as part of my very early research even though it may seem to be somewhat irrelevant.

> *A tram makes its way down Sydney Road, Melbourne. It was 1978 and Rhonda looks up at the sound of the driver's bell, "ding ding". She steps back up onto the kerb.*

Late for work again but pleasantly distracted by the encounter on the weekend passed.

She spent most of Saturday evening talking to a nice young boy at the dance.

Not who she went with, but a nice boy.

She had stars in her eyes.

He was handsome, fit and very athletic in build.

He told her how he was studying to become an airline pilot.

Determined to become a pilot.

She was impressed by his focus and passion.

During the official post-incident DoT interview, Rhonda had somewhat innocently and naïvely related what Fred had said to her one night while they were parked at the top car park of Mount Dandenong. In her words as per the DoT report, Fred had said, "If a UFO landed in front of me now, I would go in it, but never without you."

Lovers talk … and who would blame them?

The investigators' note incorrectly states that they were driving around Mt Dandenong but Rhonda was clear that they were parked in the top carpark at the time, overlooking Melbourne.

This was taken completely out of the context under which it was uttered and was submitted in the report notes as supposedly added proof of Fred's instability and his alleged pre-occupation with UFOs.

To date, there has been absolutely no evidence to support that theory, and neither was it ever proven to me to be the case by anyone who I have ever spoken to who knew Fred well.

From what I gathered, he had a typical interest in UFOs given the headline offerings in the cinemas of the day, but it was a response that was quite common when I ever enquired about Fred and the type of character he was perceived to be.

Rhonda freely admits to occasionally discussing the subject with Fred, but as to whether or not he ever did have a scrapbook on UFOs, well, she is adamant that she had never seen it.

It would be fair to say the investigators were endeavouring to set him up as a "conspiracy theorist", capitalising on his supposed obsession with UFOs.

And what's more amazing is that by and large, their campaign worked.

How preposterous that even to this day, this information still forms the backbone of any in-depth analysis into Fred's mental state and disposition.

All those years ago, I myself had ceased enquiries on account of all the negative feedback that came my way from whoever I asked about the incident. All this at the time when Steven Spielberg's box office hit *Close Encounters of the Third Kind* and the first *Star Wars* movies had not long before been released here in Australia.

Although released after Fred's disappearance, it was also the time of other groundbreaking movies like *E.T.* and the sci-fi horror *Alien*, and we were all smitten to some degree by the new genre.

If you were there, then you would understand and recall the excitement and hype surrounding that novel cinematic sci-fi era, and it was commonplace to discuss UFOs and outer space.

The following investigator's note is titled "Investigator's Assessment of Miss Rushton". It is the investigator's "summary" of Rhonda and is reproduced in its entirety as follows:

> *Miss Rushton was considered by the investigator to be an honest and reliable witness. Although young she was seen as a stable person for her years. She obviously cared greatly for Valentich and in the time of her acquaintance was proud to be associated with him, as a pilot and because of his physique and his association with the Victorian Squadron of the Air Training Corps. To some extent this shows a measure of her being impressionable, but not outside of her years.*

The investigator gained the impression that Valentich had chosen Miss Rushton carefully, as someone to discuss his problems with, she being receptive, perhaps more so than a girl of 18–20 years, who might have rejected his problems and ideas and pushed him aside.

The impression was gained that Miss Rushton was becoming aware that Valentich was "different" from her other male acquaintances and that she was being used as a "prop", based on the phrase used and the tone of some of her comments.

J.C. Sandercock
Investigator

The report is presumptuous, endeavouring to "lead" the reader by inferring that Fred was in some way attempting to "groom" Rhonda, a 16-year-old girl, assuming that she was impressionable, vulnerable and someone who had simply been smitten by Fred's physique.

Rhonda loved Fred and nothing could be further from the truth. The suggestion that Rhonda thought that Fred was "different" and was using her as a "prop" was based solely upon that interviewer's own perceptions.

Significantly, Rhonda had also told me of the humiliating personal questions that she had been made to endure on the day of her interview with the DoT, and that even now she was too affronted to relate the actual context or nature of those questions.

Suffice to say, they were extremely personal and of a sexual nature and from all I had seen, these questions had been omitted in the official transcript of the interview. This in itself is a separate matter and can be interpreted as editing of a legal transcript, most likely as a result of their questioning being wholly inappropriate.

Nothing was off the table and nothing was sacred, being asked of a 16-year-old girl who was being questioned alone and without representation.

I am struggling to refine a position on this that would sit well with this report.

What does all of this tell us about the modus operandi of the interviewing team and of the direction that they wanted the whole enquiry to ultimately head as they were seemingly fixed on delivering a pre-determined verdict rather than seeking to gain one by investigation?

After Rhonda and I spoke about the interview and the way she had felt emotionally ill-equipped and intimidated in the presence of the investigators, she paused and said, "But there's one more thing I'd like to say about the interview."

For two hours, she hadn't even clearly been able to see the faces of her interviewers, as they were all behind bright lights which were pointed directly at her.

Again, what does that kind of setup tell us about the intentions of the interviewers? Certainly, they were not concerned about creating a relaxing atmosphere of openness and fairness.

How intimidating must that have been for a 16-year-old girl, especially one who was already suffering from the emotional loss of the love of her life, and it's quite apparent with the benefit of hindsight that is exactly what Fred was to Rhonda.

Rhonda had spoken of the emotional trauma of losing Fred, and how she recalled she hadn't been able to stop crying for weeks after that loss. The pressure of the enquiry and the media coverage were factors in this.

Either intentionally or subconsciously, it was very revealing on their part. There can be no doubt that the interviewers in that room knew exactly what they were doing that day when they purposefully choreographed the cold, intimidating environment in which to conduct the interview, and also that there had been a foregone "conclusion" in their minds prior to the meeting that day.

But maybe not an actual conclusion, because a conclusion implies that a pathway of reasoning and deliberation had been undertaken, with a view to obtain a finding based upon impartiality, but this was not the case.

At the time of Fred's disappearance, Rhonda was 16 years of age (not 17 as incorrectly stated in the report), which is the legal age of consent in Victoria and has been since 1883, but she was still legally a minor, having not reached the age of 18 years.

From my understanding, the law is complicated in situations like this. Given that Rhonda was of the legal age of consent, the line of questioning was conceivably based upon investigating whether or not Fred and Rhonda's relationship had been sexually consensual.

It is the only reason that I can see that such a line of questioning would have been pursued by the investigative team, that being the sexual activity between herself, a minor of 16 years of age, and Fred, a 20-year-old male.

Rhonda has always been very guarded about the specific nature of the questions she had been asked during that interrogation, because that's what it was, other than to say that they were of such a deeply personal nature and she wouldn't even repeat them, which says enough in itself.

In any event, they either were unsuccessful in establishing that case during the course of their inquiry or, for whatever reason, they just couldn't obtain enough of the right information to make that charge stick.

Alternatively, was it simply that such accusations, if made public, would have just been a bridge too far, and because of their obvious irrelevancy to the case at hand, may have set off alarm bells in the community as to the real motive of the investigators?

What other reason would there be, could there be, for adopting such a line in their questioning toward her, a mere bystander on the whole scene and seemingly totally removed from solving the question of a missing person?

But if they were pursuing that agenda in the desire to discredit Fred, and it would seem obvious to me that they were, then I would think that they were conducting an illegal interview with an unaccompanied minor, and so perhaps their legal advice was that any information gained from that interrogation would have ultimately been inadmissible.

Paradoxically, by questioning a 16-year-old female alone and without either parental consent or proper representation. They had contravened the rules of the same law that they were seemingly conspiring to use against Fred, that being to do with the rights of a minor.

From what I can determine, the moment had passed for them because in any subsequent interview, no accompanying adult would have ever allowed such questioning to proceed unchallenged.

Such was their determination to undermine the credibility of young Fred, and if this is true, if my hunch is correct, then the investigators had come to the table with dirty hands … and it's unethical nasty stuff.

It all confirms what I've suspected and alluded to from the start. It was never actually just about a missing plane and a missing pilot. It was more about keeping a lid on the whole incident and the media flurry that had sprung up around it; an incident of a missing aircraft involving a UFO, and it was a story that was both gathering momentum and gaining unwanted worldwide attention.

18

The engagement ring and plans for the future

According to Rhonda, she and Fred were very much in love and were preparing to share a life together. So much so, when he was away, he wrote to her as often as every second day and was always the gentleman, opening doors for her wherever they went.

The 20th of every month was their anniversary, and Fred would mark it with dinner out and often a special gift.

On the night of their third monthly anniversary, Fred booked a night at Troika Restaurant and even arranged for a violinist to play for them at their table.

They had been taking dancing lessons for six weeks in preparation for their planned wedding night which, granted, was still some time away but it is quite apparent that Fred was in love and deeply committed to Rhonda.

He was shaping up to be a heck of a guy in my estimation.

Fred was impatient and had also bought a friendship ring, secretly proposing to her at the car park at the top of Mt Dandenong on the night of Friday, October 13th.

Rhonda had willingly accepted his offer of marriage and it is clear to me from that point on, Rhonda and Fred were engaged.

This ring was in place of the actual engagement ring, which was still on "lay-by" until Christmas of that year. In the meantime, it would be proof of his intentions and his love for her on their monthly anniversary, which was to fall on the following Friday, the 20th.

However, in the investigators' notes of the interview with Rhonda, particular reference was made to the purchase of the friendship ring, describing it as being "one strange thing", noting that it had been given to her a week prior to the date of their monthly anniversary. Could it be taken that the investigator was inferring that Fred had wanted Rhonda to have something to remember him by after he had disappeared? Or else why give it prominence in the report? It is doubtful that he may have been suggesting that the gift of a friendship ring was inconsistent with their theory of suicide.

It should be remembered that the gift of a friendship ring was more commonplace then than now, and to this end, the ring was proof of Fred's love for Rhonda and not just something for her to remember him by after he was gone.

Fred had told Rhonda that he wanted to announce their engagement to the family at Christmas in 1978, with a plan to marry after he had turned 21 in June 1979 and after she had turned 18 later that year.

As stated, they had both been invited to Grandy's house for drinks the evening of the following day, being Saturday, October 21st, after Fred had returned from his planned King Island flight.

Ronald had thought a lot of Fred and often invited him over to his family home to socialise. According to Rhonda, he was deeply affected by Fred's disappearance, later confiding in her that Fred was "commonsense on two legs" and that he would "have a big problem finding a replacement for Fred". It is obvious that there was a very strong mutual bond between the two men.

As Rhonda said, Fred was a planner and an old-fashioned kind of guy. He was a gentleman who believed in flowers, violins and opening doors for his lady. He was a quality guy and obviously a hard act for someone to follow as a replacement in Rhonda's life.

Staying with this whole theme, it's quite reasonable to assume that Fred may have been wearing his Air Force uniform on the day he flew to King Island so as to look the part for drinks at Grandy's that evening.

Through it all, despite some challenges, it must have been such a wonderful time for both of them.

Rhonda was welcomed with open arms by the family. According to Rhonda, Fred's mother, Alberta, was fully onboard too, as she was the person who willingly took Fred's cash payments for the engagement ring into the little jewellery store every week.

The engagement ring was on "lay-by" at a jeweller's shop in Puckle Street, Moonee Ponds, a northern suburb of Melbourne. He had planned to have it paid off before Christmas 1978, at which time he would already be 20 years of age and Rhonda would have turned 17.

In all of this, I don't see a man contemplating suicide. I see a man contemplating life.

I see a strong, unbreakable lifelong relationship being forged between the two of them, with Rhonda being the love of his young life, someone he could talk to and confide in, just the way any strong relationship should be.

By their action or inaction, the investigators have denied her the memory of all that was good about their relationship, and in so doing have denied Rhonda the closure she was entitled to and the chance for her to move on with her life. Later in life, she was engaged three times and, by her own admission, was unable to ever settle.

The whole affair, tainted by media misinformation and innuendo, had defined her character in the years that followed, and not in any good way, when it could have been, should have been, very different.

I feel that Rhonda had been wronged, and one can only imagine what the legal repercussions would have been if this had all occurred today.

Comments in the investigators' notes that accuse Fred of using Rhonda as "a bit of a prop" and that "a woman of older years would probably not have stayed with Fred" were cruel and unjustified, implying that Rhonda was naïve for having been involved in that relationship and that Fred was unnaturally insecure.

At the time, it would not have been unreasonable to have demanded an explanation for including such hurtful observations in the report notes.

Returning to the main objective: what purpose did statements like these serve in the course of an investigation into a missing person?

Fred was no stranger to the flight across Bass Strait and had previously flown to King Island on three or four occasions, but always during daytime.

He and Rhonda had originally planned to go on the flight together that day but that didn't happen. Subsequently, Fred had departed later and alone.

Fred had made no contact with Rhonda or anyone else that Saturday evening, and so strong was their bond that to her it could only have meant one thing, and she immediately feared the worst.

Rhonda spoke of how she didn't sleep that night. She just lay on top of her bed all night at her parents' house, staring out the window at the stars in the new outfit, jacket, silk blouse and slacks she had purchased especially to go to drinks at Ronald Grandy's house.

As usual, at 6 am, she heard her father in the next room turn the radio on to the ABC morning news, only to hear the lead broadcast that a pilot was missing over Bass Strait.

He called out to her from the next room, "Rhonda, did you hear that?"

Managing to find a number in the phone book, Rhonda rang Moorabbin Airport.

Screening calls, the attending duty officer asked, "Can you tell me the name of the pilot?" With halting breath, she had replied, "Frederick Valentich", to which came the immediate instruction, "Hold the line …"

She never wore that outfit again.

Rhonda and Fred

19

Steve Robey

Steve Robey was the attending Melbourne Flight Service duty officer who was on the other end of the radio to Fred during their famous six-minute conversation on the 21st of October 1978.

I originally met Steve after he had kindly invited me to the 40th anniversary of the disappearance, which took place at Moorabbin Airport in late 2018.

Steve won't offer it, but he was born in Yorkshire, England, and being a "Yorky boy" is perhaps what gives him that distinctive tonal clip in his voice, so identifiable in the original tape transcript.

I originally found Steve on Facebook and he responded almost immediately to my message.

Open and trusting, Steve had spoken to me plainly about what he thought he knew about Fred's disappearance, gleaned from the last conversation he had had with him on that fateful evening.

I also had the opportunity to meet Rhonda Rushton and a lot of the other Valentich mystery loyalists. Individuals who have kept the faith despite their frustration at knowing the truth to do with a UFO's intervention, but without ever having credibly verbalised it in so many words.

My recollection is that there were no closed doors, and as a newcomer, I was made to feel quite at home that day.

To date, it is the one and only UFO meeting that I have ever attended and regrettably, because it had been a long day, I had left early.

I have on occasion pressed Steve on what his thoughts were about the six-minute radio conversation he had with Fred. While his responses were never overt, and perhaps even somewhat muted, at the same time he is definite and unwavering.

"Yes, there was something." "Yes, I felt he was in control." He would nod. He believed that Fred was genuine and that he wasn't making it up, and on that evening, Fred had been telling the truth. Telling it exactly as he saw it.

A pilot himself and given the years of talking and listening to pilots under various levels of stress as a Flight Service Officer, he is very aware of the pressures of the cockpit.

His testimony and his opinion on that one point are, to me, both worthy and coveted.

Steve's voice is unmistakably recognisable in the original recording of the radio conversation between Frederick Valentich and himself, and so is forever inextricably linked with one of the world's great aviation mysteries.

If it is any consolation at all, then it can be said that at the very least, Fred had a professional and measured response at the other end of the microphone for his last conversation on this earth, regardless of whatever one's interpretation of the final outcome may be.

Steve Robey passed away on the 16th of August 2025.

Rhonda Rushton and Steve Robey. 2018

20

Merv O'Meara

Merv O'Meara was born in 1938 in Apollo Bay, Victoria, where he worked and lived all his life.

For the last 12 years of his working life, he was employed as Harbourmaster at Apollo Bay.

He was married to Pat and they had three children, two boys and a girl.

During my time at Apollo Bay, I had heard the story of someone who also lived in the town who witnessed an aircraft in company with a UFO while driving home along the Barham River road, just behind Apollo Bay, but in 20 years, I had never met him.

This was curious given that the population of Apollo Bay is about fifteen hundred people and that I was the local pilot. But when considering this further, it is entirely consistent with his lifestyle subsequent to going public with his report of having witnessed an aeroplane and UFO. By his own volition, he had very much faded from public view.

According to Merv, on that evening, he had his two sons, his daughter and his niece Tracie in the car with him. It was right on dark and they were travelling home to the township of Apollo Bay after a day out rabbiting up the Barham River road.

I recorded two interviews with him on the 22nd of September 2018, one at his home and one actually out onsite, where the sighting had taken place. This allowed me to gain a full appreciation of both the geography and the perspectives involved.

The following are transcripts of those recorded interviews.

Interview 1 with Merv O'Meara was recorded with his wife Pat in attendance at their home overlooking Marengo and the Barham River flats to the south.

This is Merv's account of what occurred on the evening of Frederick Valentich's disappearance.

Victor: Tell us again now, Merv, where did you say you saw the plane?

Merv: Straight out on the top of Marengo. Marengo Heights. Above that. On the Paradise Road, coming down.

V: Was that down low on Paradise Road or up high?

M: Down low I was.

V: So you were looking straight out to sea?

M: No, straight up in the hills. But coming down towards the sea. [Indicating that the plane was descending towards the sea.] You couldn't see the sea from [where we] were.

V: So you saw him across the hills?

M: Yes, I saw him up on top of the hills and one of the nieces said to me, "Look, there's a funny looking aeroplane," and when I looked, there was nothing there and I said, "I can't see anything." Anyway, I kept coming a bit further and I came over the bridge very near Cam McFee's old joint and I looked and I could see this aeroplane and I said, "That's an aeroplane." She said, "No, that's not the one I saw, there was another one." Anyway, when I looked back and there is a real round hill at the top, and it come up over that, and it came down onto the top, the plane was coming along like that, and he [UFO] was up here behind him [demonstrating with his hands] coming down towards [indistinct] and ...

V: So whatever it was, was following him?

M: Yes. And it kept going. I watched them till they disappeared, and they disappeared here, well, you can see the old dam out here [indicating], just the other side of that from where we were sitting, we saw the thing disappear behind the hills.

V: Over the top of that dam type of thing, is that what you are saying?

M: He was further over but from where we were, it was over the dam [from inside O'Meara's house] when it disappeared.

V: The only— yeah, ok, so you wouldn't have had an idea how far out or how high he was or any of that sort of stuff, could you see the detail of the plane or …?

M: Yes. I could see it clear as day.

V: Yeah, right.

M: But you couldn't see … the other thing was just a bloody big bright light.

V: What colour light do you know?

M: I thought that it was bloody, er … green light.

V: Mmm, I think he said it was green.

M: Mmm, I thought it was green and that's what they reckon he got mixed up, got mixed up with the bloke flying the plane, the young bloke, with, um … with the green lights at the harbour.

V: Oh yeah, it's a bit of a coincidence though, isn't it?

M: And they said he wasn't coming from the Otway but he was coming from the Otway! [voice elevated] – because from here and where we were, from here you look west and the Otway is more west here.

V: Yes.

M: The Otway is more west because when you go to the Otway, you turn to go …

V: Are you saying he was on the way back?

M: Yes.

V: He was on the way back.

M: Yes, from the Otway, yes.

V: So you are saying he was tracking back to Apollo Bay from when you saw him?

M: Yes, that's what it looked like to me.

V: Well, Merv, that's exactly what I wanted to hear.

M: Mmm …

V: Because that's the only scenario that would fit with everything that's occurred. He was on his way back and that thing was on his tail.

M: Yes.

V: That's crucial to this. That actually makes this fit together. Because I didn't want to bring that point out unless you admitted it.

M: Mmm …

V: Because if he was on his way down [to Cape Otway] with it on his tail, that doesn't fit. But he was on his way back, that fits.

M: Mmm … He came from the island to Cape Otway, from King Island to Cape Otway, didn't he?

V: No, he was on his way down and he was then circling, and no one knows what happened after that but you are saying that he must have turned around and came back? You're saying he was on the way back because he said—

M: Yes, he was on the way back from the Otway, because the Otway is west from here and he was coming back from that way, and he followed the bloody hills right down here … [indicating]

V: Towards Apollo Bay?

M: Yes, towards, out, Marengo Heights, that's where he … right at the back of there …

V: And that was the same night as the disappearance of Frederick.

M: Yes, that was it.

V: Ok.

M: And we didn't know until we heard it on the news, didn't we?

Pat: Yes, they [Merv and the children in the car] came and told me about this aeroplane and the light.

M: And the UFO.

P: And I didn't believe a thing he said, and the next day it was on the news.

M: And it wasn't a bloody aeroplane!

V: Did anyone interview you from the official authorities that were of the day, like the aviation department, did anyone come and see you or speak to you about that?

P: At the, er … the George River, they were making a film, but that was later, but there was two or three.

M: Oh yes, that's the bloke from America.

P: And he interviewed Merv.

M: Oh no, they had the thing, where was it around the, er … the George river … the bloke on the UFOs.

V: But no one from the department of aviation came and saw you?

M: No.

V: Ok, so, that's very typical of this whole scenario, it was very disjointed and I believe it wasn't complete. What you just told me was crucial, ahhhem, now ahm … the people who were in the car with you, they're all grown up now?

M: Oh yes.

V: Did they remember anything?

M: No, they didn't even remember a lot because they didn't go up. I can't think of that chap's name, the bloke that was on the UFO thing.

V: But getting back to it, how many were in the car with you?

M: Four, my two sons and the two girls.

V: Nieces, and who saw it?

P: Tracie.

M: Tracie saw it first, and she said to me, "Uncle Merv, there's a bright light or an aeroplane." And I looked, I couldn't see a thing, and I looked and I said, "There's nothing there." She said, "Oh well, there was." Anyway, I kept looking, I kept driving down. Anyway, I kept looking and I kept driving down, you know where Frank lives now?

V: Yes.

M: We were coming down past there and I just kept going and we got down here to the next bridge, where Neville was living at the time, and er … I looked and I said, "Oh there's the aeroplane there." She said, "No, that's not it." She said … "It was a real bright light, the one I saw."

V: Yes.

M: And it must have circled around, and I looked again and the next thing I could see it coming back, over the top of this bald looking hill there, and er … on top of, sort of on top of, behind the plane but more or less on top, and they were both going down like that together [motioning with his hands]. And as it went down, we lost sight of it out here where Ralph is living, it went down behind the hills. That's where it must have crashed up …

V: Do you know of anyone else that saw that, Merv?

M: Yes, [name withheld] saw it, didn't she? And that's where it must have crashed down there behind the hills [meaning in the ocean].

P: Yes, but she won't say because she thinks that people think she's a fool and—

M: They've got a farm out here [now sold] near the big corner.

V: Oh really, well, that's all very interesting.

P: But she sort of said nothing since because she doesn't want to get involved.

The interview stopped at 10:45 am but restarted within 10 minutes to get a quote from Merv regarding his statement.

In a general conversation that was not recorded, Merv had mentioned, uninvited, that he had witnessed them "two together". These words were a significant and precise admission on his part. There had been no intention to "lead" him in his testimony, although it could perhaps be construed that way.

V: Something you said before is very important. Had you been drinking?

M: No.

P: No.

V: No. Tell us again, you used a phrase that's relevant to this enquiry. "Two together"? Tell us again about that.

M: Yes, whatever the other thing was, it wasn't an aeroplane.

V: But there were two together.

M: Yes.

V: Ok.

M: But the one at the top was probably a hundred feet above the bloody plane. The thing at the back.

V: So it was that close?

M: Well, that's what it looked like from where we were.

V: It's hard to know, isn't it?

M: Yes, it is.

V: And you're saying it was just above the hills.

M: Yes, well, that's what it looked like from where we were, because we were down low on this road here, and they were up on the top, on the ocean road.

V: And he was making his way to Melbourne.

M: No, he looked like he was flying back toward Blanket Bay – no, not Blanket Bay, the Elliot [River].

V: Well, which way was he going when you saw him?

M: He was coming from the west, which would be from the Otway Lighthouse, and he was coming this way.

V: Ok, yes, yes. So that's the same, he was flying back this way. Ok, so he was flying back this way, yes, that's what I meant.

M: But not right to Apollo Bay, they were out off the Elliot or one of those places there.

V: Right.

M: Because that's where the plane went down, wasn't it? Off er …

V: I don't know, I don't know, they couldn't find anything. I mean, I think that this is crucial if you saw a plane at that point and no one interviewed you from the authorities. I thought, *That's pretty amazing.*

M: Mmm …

V: But you know what? – it was well known around town that you had seen something because I heard about it a couple of times, that Merv had seen it.

M: Mmm …

V: You know and yet no one bothered to come and see you about it.

M: And as I say, everybody reckoned it was rubbish, you know, but it wasn't, something definitely put him down.

End of Interview 1.

Interview 2 was held onsite approximately an hour later with Merv out on Barham River Road, about three kilometres out of Apollo Bay and travelling eastwards back toward Apollo Bay to where Merv had sighted the light plane in company with the UFO.

V: Ok, Merv. Just travelling east, big bald hill on our right. Where did you see it?

M: Just down here a bit further the other side of this hill and up through that gully.

V: Yes.

M: This is where she first saw it. These trees have grown since.

V: Yes. Sure.

M: That's where she would have seen it first up. She first saw it there and when I looked, I couldn't see anything. There was nothing.

V: Yes.

M: So I said, "No, I can't see anything," and she said, "Oh, I can't see it now either."

V: Yes.

M: So we kept going.

V: How old would she have been then?

M: Oh, I don't think she would have been a teenager then. No, she wouldn't have been.

V: So coming down here.

M: Then she sees it again. She says there's the light, and I couldn't see it. Anyway, I went a bit further, here at Neville's drive right here, that's when I looked and that's when I saw the aeroplane. And I said, "It's an aeroplane," and she said, "No, not that, it was back there." Anyway, I went to drive on a little bit more now.

V: Just for the record, we are parked on the driveway at 200 Barham River Road where Merv is saying the second sighting occurred by Tracie, his niece, and then what did you say?

M: Yes. And I stopped just here, and I could still see the plane, and I said, "That's an aeroplane," and she said, "No, not that. Look back there!" … "And when I looked back there, that's when the light came out from behind the big hill, the bald hill. It came over nearly on top of the plane.

V: Over here on our right.

M: Yes. The plane started to go down, going down, and the light was following it.

V: Ok, we are looking back in a south-easterly direction, and the plane was travelling which direction?

M: Straight along that hill. Following that hill. It was going east. Or a little bit southeast.

V: So it was heading back towards the township of Apollo Bay, would you agree with that?

M: Yes, well, it was going more to the Elliot. [The Elliot River over the hill on the coast.]

V: More to the Elliot.

M: Yes.

V: Right, so just to clarify this, it was heading this way?

M: No, it was heading that way. The way we are facing now.

V: Ok, yes, ok, but what I mean was it wasn't going west?

M: No.

V: It was heading more east? Ok, that would have taken it more offshore maybe, do you think?

M: Offshore? No, it would be still following the coast.

V: Following the coast, let me just go [zoom] out here. [Referencing the vehicle's GPS display.]

M: It would be more southeast the way we are facing now.

V: Ok, so there we are.

M: That's where the Marengo Heights here and that's where the plane was heading there. That'd be more to the right of Marengo [relatively speaking, from our current location] where it went down to the Elliot, or the Parker, one of the two.

V: Ah, now the Parker and the Elliot.

M: The Elliot is first, Ralph's and then you've got the Parker next to it.

V: So, the plane was heading, that's north there. What direction do you think the plane was travelling, Merv?

M: Travelling, oh east, southeast.

V: Yes, ok. Yes. And how high above those trees would it have been, Merv?

M: It was up fairly high there, would have been a couple of hundred feet up, easy, probably more.

V: See that bird there.

M: Yes, would be a bit higher than that.

V: And you could identify it as a plane?

M: Oh yes. Easy. Yes.

V: But then there was the other phenomena?

M: Yes, but it was a bit higher than it, and I'm sure it was just one big bright green light.

V: Right, right.

M: And we kept going down here.

V: Yep. Travelling back down the Barham Road.

M: And across here, out where the … the airstrip is.

V: Yes, over the top of the airstrip.

M: Towards the airstrip, that's when it disappeared. We couldn't see it for that, the hills of the ocean road.

V: Heading down?

M: Yes, it was still heading down.

V: And heading out in a …?

M: Out to sea. Yes.

V: Was the light in appearance at that point?

M: Yes. They were both together, the plane was there and the big light behind was there, and they were just going along like that, together [motioning].

V: Ok.

M: Ralph's straight across there. There's a lot more trees there now, on bloody Heathfield [Estate]. They have planted heaps of trees. That was all vacant then, Old Sparrow Newcombe had it then. It was all a farm. But see all these trees here weren't here. All the ones on Heathfield.

V: Ok thanks, Merv.

Interview 2 was paused.

V: Say it again, er … just re-starting this interview. I'm parked at the top of the hill near David's place on the Great Ocean Road. [At that point, we had driven around to the coast, approximately four kilometres out of Apollo Bay and approximately two kilometres up the hill west from the Marengo airfield.] Umm … where did you say that the plane disappeared, Merv?

M: Down through the gully here at the Elliot. I reckon it come in behind and went into the drink at the Elliot or the Parker.

V: Next to what's-his-name?

M: Ralph.

V: Ralph's place?

M: Yes.

V: Right, ok, he's heading in an east-southeasterly direction at that point?

M: Yes.

V: He's on descent and heading back it would seem from his trip to King Island according to the witness.

End of Interview 2.

It has been said that writing a book is like having children. You don't contemplate the second one until you've forgotten the pain of the first.

The assembly of the facts can be painful and presenting them in a coherent, logical way is challenging.

Thankfully, I had taken the time to interview Merv back in 2018 for his critical account of what he saw on the evening of the 21st of October 1978.

Sadly, he did not live to see the result of his witness statement come to fruition, nor will he ever see the result of the trust that he placed in me in being so open and forthright in his testimony.

During the course of my enquiries about Frederick Valentich, I can say with regret that many weren't so open.

It's not easy to ask something of someone and expect that they will be forthcoming to a complete stranger about a long-past and controversial event.

I'm sure that there would have been many opportunities for Merv to tell his story and also that there were, according to him, many not-so-positive encounters in the form of hurtful sarcasm and negativity.

Australians are some of the most welcoming and companionable people on earth, especially in times of hardship and adversity, but they can also be some of the cruellest.

Their expertise at sardonic humour is well-entrenched, and even though I dislike the phrase, they are well-practised in the art of Tall Poppy Syndrome. "You're fine, mate, just don't try and stand out above the rest of us."

I grew up in hotels among working-class Australians and I know something about this. And it isn't restricted to our own culture.

Some people unknowingly throw hurtful terms and phrases about with impunity. These terms, such as "conspiracy theorist", "anti-vaxxer" and even the more benign term "bigshot", innocent as they may seem, can prevent any chance of constructive conversation ever occurring.

Put-downs are destructive. They require no skill at all and they are so easy to keep in the toolbox of hurtful retort, handing power to those who crave it.

Someone has a laugh, but then that concept or that observation is consigned to the dark emotional recesses of the mind of the individual who originally may have openly proffered it.

Critical thinking, or even just truth-telling, wasn't always a valued trait in our culture, a culture that was immersed in the mindset of plain hard work and the long, unforgiving day.

Merv O'Meara found himself grappling with this and the hurt of criticisms of his colleagues and mates, choosing eventually not to talk about what he saw or even to not visit the hotel as frequently as before.

By his own admission, he wasn't as comfortable in his hometown anymore as he made his way through those years. But he never relented, never forgot and never ever conceded that he had seen an illusion or had suffered an aberration.

It would have been far easier to just forget, to consign it to the past and re-join the everyday rank and file, taking his lunch to work and not challenging the established and the known. In essence, "not to rock the boat" because it is both an unfortunate fact that being open and forthright when innocently recalling an event and then in turn espousing an opinion can be interpreted as a threat.

People often dislike someone who displays such a mindset because it challenges them personally and speaks to them of the person that they always wanted to be but weren't, never themselves having had the substance or the will to observe, to be critical, and to challenge.

I found my short time with Merv O'Meara, my brief entry into the other world of the inconceivable, to be transformative, galvanising a burning commitment within me to complete this book.

As I listened to his story and noted the directness of his words and the intensity of his expression, I could only be thankful that he took the time and was trusting enough to pass the baton as I mentally downloaded all the information and the uniqueness of the moment.

I feel he knew his life's journey was finite and, on that day, he entrusted me as the new courier of something he had been internalising for so long. A very special experience.

I feel that on that day, he said to me, "Take it, and do with it what I couldn't."

Recalling his face when he looked at me and said those simple, uncompromising words, "I know what I saw."

It was perhaps not obvious to me at the time but with the benefit of hindsight, it is very apparent that I was then bestowed with the responsibility to move forward with that knowledge and to somehow re-ignite the flame, from the small flicker of whatever still existed in the spirit of his aging person.

I wasn't consulted. It was in effect a fait accompli that had occurred between two men who had met because they were destined to meet. This story would not have been told unless we had met, and the importance of Merv's eyewitness account had been made apparent to me.

I have decided that I will not let this small but highly significant piece of history – not just that of Fred and Merv's history, but Australian history – fade away and be lost; I would be the courier of that message.

Although it has been years since that interview, I remember it well and re-listening to his voice as he speaks of the encounter engenders a very powerful memory in me, the memory of his truthfulness. So, I undertake to give his testimony the oxygen that it requires to burn bright.

In saying that, I reflect on a quote from Ross Coulthard: "There is an obligation to the facts, not just the facts as they sit, but in the responsibility of arranging and relaying those facts to not only make them comprehensible, but to also ensure that they are digestible."

That can be painful.

It is a responsibility and just like all responsibilities, in a perfect world, they are something we would dream of being rid of. Something to be completely retired from.

There is responsibility in the act of writing: the need to get it right and more so if it's something you value, something in which there is a personal stake.

Mervyn O'Meara passed away on the 26th of January 2023.

He was 85 years of age.

Merv O'Meara

21

The elephant in the room

Pat O'Meara recently thanked me over the telephone, and just as I thought we had covered all the bases and loose ends to do with her late husband, Merv, she offered as a parting comment, "Yes, well, you know we had the boy's father here a number of times. He used to like to come and talk to Merv."

"The boy's father? Fred's father, Guido?"

"Yes, he came here three or four times to talk with Merv."

Pat's innocent comments had re-opened a door of realisation, something that I had already previously been aware of.

Of course he did. The two men had known each other, and I had known that.

I had also mentioned that fact in my 2018 email to the ATSB and NASA, but at the time, I hadn't fully realised the significance of that relationship to this investigation.

It had been lost and forgotten in my mind among the brambles and briars of the other significant and insignificant facts yet to be collated and arranged.

Guido Valentich, who died in 2000, was a regular visitor to the lighthouse and especially on the anniversary of Fred's disappearance. He believed his son would one day return or be returned.

Now it wasn't only about Fred's survival, but also about the survival and hope for both himself, and his family.

Unbeknownst to Guido, it was a hope based on a flawed investigation, forcing him as a parent to forever endure the unspeakable pain of a lost child and of never knowing. So, quite conceivably, these visits to the O'Meara household had become his last source of solace, helping him grapple with that whole experience.

Why hadn't anyone in the DoT ever questioned Merv? There was no reference to him at all in the witness statements or any of the investigators' documents released under FOI. If there were any references to Merv, then they weren't apparent in any of the investigators' notes that I had read.

If these references had been withheld from the available FOI files, was it because they were perhaps too revealing of an obvious lack of action in the face of all the available evidence?

I outlined Merv's sighting in my 2018 letter to BASI and was rebuffed with words to the effect of, any information coming forth after so many years cannot be relied upon and that with respect to aviation safety, they choose to save their resources for more relevant matters.

The question is: was that a response based upon that organisation's mission statement, or was it based on a directive from above?

But the question remains; while it would be reasonable to assume that Guido Valentich knew all about the witness of Merv O'Meara and the full context of that account, who else would have known?

Guido would have been ground zero as interviewees go. He was the mouthpiece and the touchstone for all authorities to do with Fred's disappearance, and his name had been mentioned many times in their documentation.

My considered opinion is that, as an Italian immigrant, Guido would never have chosen to rock the boat by questioning the authority of the day. Most likely he would have naively followed the path of least resistance, trusting them and choosing to take them entirely at their word when they had assured him that they had the situation fully under control.

In all of this it would be unrealistic to think that Guido had not informed them of Merv's existence and of his eyewitness account.

It wasn't a matter of whether Merv could have been telling the truth or not, but rather that no one had even bothered to interview him.

However you look at it, someone just wasn't doing their job or had chosen not to.

Locating the lost aeroplane with the benefit of Merv's testimony would confirm that testimony. It would also confirm what I think the authorities just couldn't deal with, or were instructed not to deal with, that being the testimony of the existence of a UFO; that is, the other craft in the drama, the one that had been pursuing Fred that evening and the one that he had spoken of in his last conversation with Melbourne Flight Service Officer Steve Robey.

In this case, they couldn't have one without the other, and as such, it couldn't be ignored. It was an embarrassment. An inconvenience.

It was the elephant in the room.

The fact that Fred was being stalked and pursued, for whatever reason, is to me confirmed, given the quality of various witness statements and given the frequency of UFO sightings throughout that region at the time.

Pursued by what and for what reason is not known, and it's fair to say will never be known. But just that there was a sighting of an aeroplane, in that location, on that night and that there was another player involved is beyond reasonable doubt.

So the big question remains as to the mindset of the investigators as revealed by their underachieving and inaction on the matter.

By dictating their own secret agenda, they had breached the trust of what was then a very trusting, naïve post-war population.

With the benefit of hindsight and of settling thoughts, this has become all too clear to me over the years, and it smells, really smells.

Very plainly, it speaks loudly of those who, for whatever reason, have deliberately and wilfully chosen not to see, and in doing so have much to answer for in having been the cause of much heartache, suffering and loss of sleep along the way.

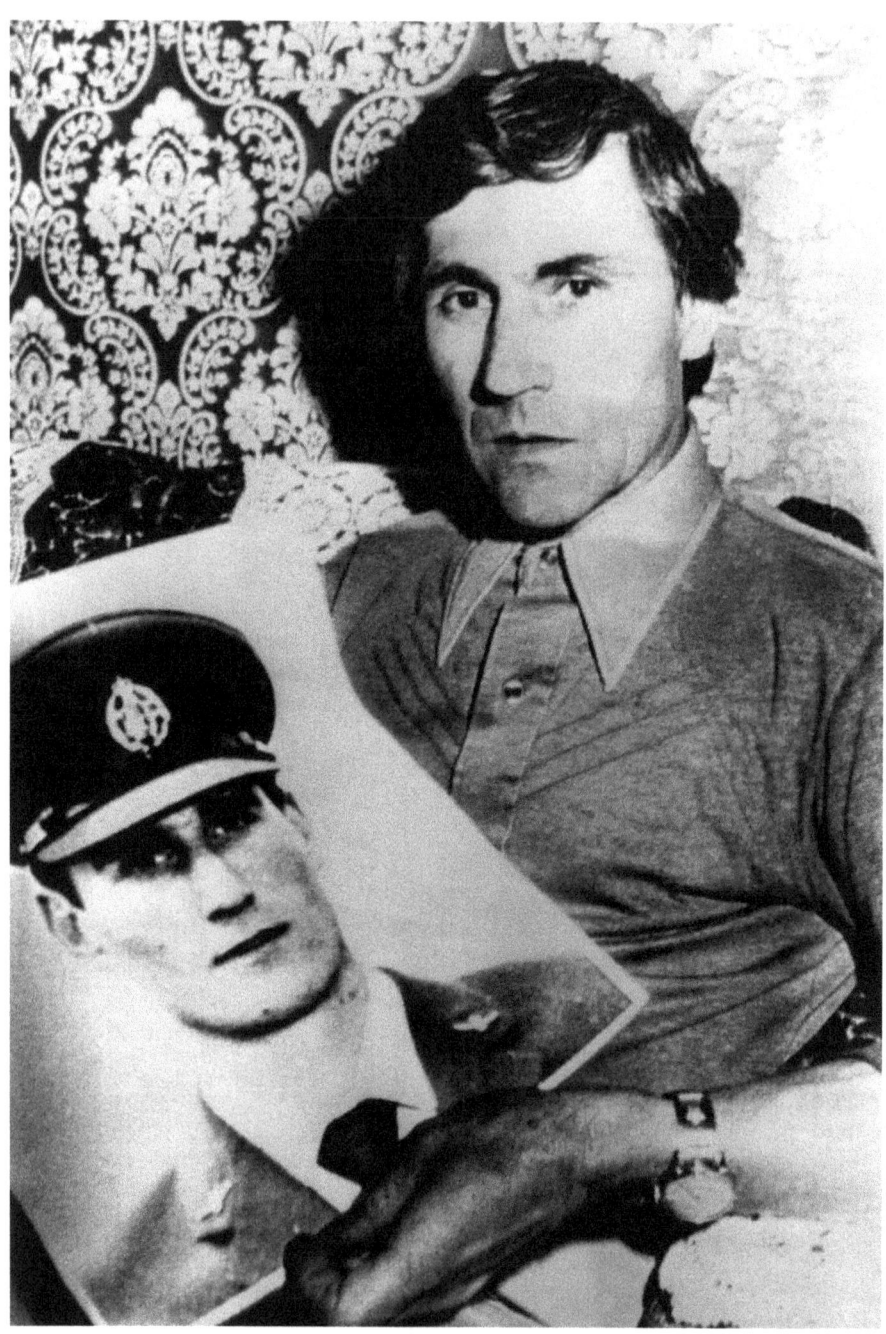

Guido Valentich holding a photo of his son Frederick. (Getty images)

By not willingly and openly assisting, as was their job for which they were paid to do, they have not allowed loved ones the closure that they were entitled to.

That information may have turned the heads of the searchers all those years ago and pointed to a logical conclusion, ultimately towards an answer and a location for an aircraft and pilot that had so mysteriously disappeared without a trace.

In this case, choosing "not to see" could be defined as either professional incompetence, professional negligence or complicity. Which will it be?

When facts are being so clearly ignored it's never because of incompetence.

I choose complicity.

Politicians and regulators alike are accountable to the law they uphold, and given the inherent responsibilities of those authorities, past and present, they should be held accountable for each and every breach of that same law.

It's only fair, and it's not too late.

22

John

The events of my life have progressively defined this book, and so it is my life that is directing the inspiration, passion and research. These elements are almost impossible to separate, and so forgive me when I speak of seemingly unrelated things to that of the disappearance of a lone pilot.

It's not so much the places on that journey that I remember as much as I do the people.

During the winter months at Apollo Bay, when charter work had tailed off and the Great Ocean Road had gone quiet – when "the fish weren't running" as I used to put it – I concentrated on my winter business in outback South Australia where the sandhills of the central deserts replaced the heaving rollers of the Great Southern Ocean.

Based in an old sandstone post office at Hawker in the Flinders Ranges, depending upon the prevailing wind, it was a four-hour flight from Apollo Bay, or a convenient 13-hour drive.

In winter months, when the heat of the South Australian summer had abated, giving way to the cool, clear desert mornings, it became a second home.

Part of my workday included names like Lake Eyre, William Creek, Birdsville, Innamincka, the Burke and Wills Dig Tree and the various bush airstrips where we would share the hospitality of the station people.

They were wonderful years and besides the magnificent remoteness, I miss the regulars, those who were themselves shaped by that remoteness.

Perhaps there was a subconscious connection with matters rural, born out of my own experience in the Western District of Victoria and the remoteness of that place.

As the self-appointed caretaker of the Burke and Wills "Dig Tree" in far western Queensland, Alfred "Bomber" Johnson was a standout to me as an person and as an aviator and so he is worthy of a special mention here. He was S. Kidman and Co's chief pilot for many years, and he had logged 7,000 flying hours in that job and some 19,000 hours in total in some of the remotest country on earth, well before GPS and mobile phones. He flew by compass, following a pencil line on a map.

In 2013, an unexpected and concerning phone call from Karen Percy of the ABC sought permission to use a photo of Bomber and myself which they had turned up online. I was then informed that, sadly, his funeral was happening as we spoke out at Eromanga, Western Queensland.

His Obituary reads:

JOHNSON, Alfred "Bomber"
M.B.E.

Bush Pilot, Dig Tree Ranger and Storyteller

It made specific mention of the fact that Bomber had been awarded the British Empire Medal, the highest civilian peacetime award available.

Myself with Alfred 'Bomber' Johnson and Rappatap.
(Bush Pilot, Storyteller)

I knew little of his personal history, other than the fact that he'd been a pilot and that he was a storyteller, which was quite evident.

What I was also aware of was that he had a quality about him, something unsaid. He was a man that you naturally gravitated towards, trusted and always believed.

That day, I placed a phone call through to S. Kidman and Co, explaining that I would like to buy the old Cessna that Bomber had flown for all those years. From what I understood, it was sitting languishing on an outback station. I was immediately put through to Managing Director Greg Campbell, who declined my offer and explained that there were plans afoot to suspend it from the roof in the Stockman's Hall of Fame in Longreach, Queensland.

It was apparent that there was a deep unspoken respect for this man who was living out his years with his old dog at remote Nappa Merrie Station in far Western Queensland, and I wondered how history will choose to remember any of us when our time comes.

Stopovers at the Dig Tree always ran behind schedule when Bomber drove over from the nearby homestead in his old utility together with his faithful red healer dog, Rappatap.

On those days, my party was always late for lunch at the Innamincka Hotel, which was only a few minutes west by air, conveniently following the Cullyamurra Waterhole in along the Cooper Creek.

Single and never married, I loved his company and his many colourful stories about the bush and the people of the bush, and so did my passengers.

I was honoured to have met him on those few brief occasions.

Vale Bomber.

He was 80 years of age.

John reminds me very much of Bomber, he's that kind of person, sincere and direct and his willingness and eagerness to tell me what he'd witnessed from the hill up behind Cape Otway and is a primary witness in these testimonies. A person that I had immediately trusted when he tells it and says, "it is", then I am sure that it is.

At the time, he was 31 years of age and working as an earthmoving contractor in the steep, dangerous hills of the Cape Otway hinterland.

On the night of October 21st, together with a work colleague, they had stopped work about 6:30 pm, and were leaning on the bulldozer having a beer before heading home when they saw a green light moving around the sky out over Bass Strait beyond Cape Otway.

They had watched it for about half an hour, and John also felt it was important to mention the strange atmosphere that evening that had accompanied the sighting, being akin to an electrical charge in the air.

This is very common in eyewitness accounts of UFO sightings, not just of those that I have read but also those that I have come to know from people who have volunteered information, face to face, unprompted and uninvited. John was one of these.

I felt guilty that for some years I had been strumming the same tune of my intention to write a book, that my motivation to write a book on the disappearance of lone pilot Frederick Valentich had been seen as commonplace and static by some Apollo Bay locals, and that this long-awaited book will never be written.

So, when I reconnect with those who are on my list, those who are still alive, it was normal for me to observe that they were becoming bored with the prospect of another interview.

I am pleased that I have waited until now, as it has given me time to evaluate more thoroughly the evidence to do with Fred's disappearance.

I re-interviewed John with his wife, Chris, and his message to me during our last conversation hadn't faded with time at all, nor lost any of its conviction. Instead, it seemed stronger than ever.

According to John, who was in company with one other that evening, the light bore no resemblance to Aurora Australis, which he was familiar with, having witnessed it on various occasions while at sea.

This sighting complements the other sightings previously noted and, in particular, that of the log entry in the Cape Otway Lighthouse keeper's journal.

Just like Merv O'Meara, strengthened through the commitment down the years and only too aware of the ravages of time, he had said to me with some conviction and a handshake and upon parting, "Vic, write this. Don't wait. It really needs to be said."

23

Mick

Michael is an old Apollo Bay local and part of the woodwork in that town.

I would more than likely run into him at the Apollo Bay Bakery when he was buying his morning "smoko" or a takeaway coffee.

I would like to think we were two men with a friendly, mutual respect for each other. Typically, he would be going out as I would be going in.

In the words of the Australian poet Henry Lawson, we were "two blokes who would meet G'day and would part G'day" but no doubt his brief testimony was very relevant and of considerable importance. More than he probably realised.

According to Michael, he was a kid camped out at Blanket Bay (between Apollo Bay and Cape Otway) with the family when he saw a light plane fly past, headed southwest along the coast towards Cape Otway.

As an uninvited comment, he also added that it was "still quite light", which fits with my assessment of the flying conditions that Fred encountered.

Also, his father mentioned that Ernie Evans, a local who at the time had owned a shack down at Blanket Bay, later told him that "he noticed a light plane going towards the Otway" and "a bit later heard a plane going back the other way".

Over the years, no other aircraft have ever been reported to me as being in the area and one must also appreciate that at that time, light aircraft traffic was less common and still somewhat of a novelty.

It is reasonable to therefore assume that it was Fred's plane that Ernie had heard passing on those occasions.

This is a brief but relevant testimony that fits with all that I know about the pattern of the last minutes of the flight path that Frederick Valentich's aircraft took back towards Apollo Bay that evening.

It is also in keeping with the timing of Merv O'Meara's sighting just off Marengo, which, concurrent in the timeline, would have occurred a couple of minutes later.

Michael apologised to me that his account was a bit low on detail, but I was grateful and thanked him for his trouble.

24

Roy Manifold

I didn't know Roy Manifold but I knew something of what had befallen him, and it seemed like it wasn't a type of fame but more a type of fate.

His experience gained worldwide attention.

Roy was camped at the shacks which at the time existed on the coast near Cape Otway, looking out to the southeast. On the evening of Fred's disappearance, he had reportedly heard an aircraft pass by.

He was an amateur photographer and was taking a series of time exposures of the sunset on the evening of Fred's disappearance.

After developing the photos, he later discovered that he had taken a photo of a mystery object in the sky, which sparked a worldwide controversy, from Cape Otway to Cape Canaveral, as NASA weighed in on the controversy.

According to the photo analysis undertaken by NASA, the analogue photo had not been altered or tampered with in any way, nor was it the result of accidental double exposure.

While the mystery airborne object in the photo has as much as possible been determined to be that of a genuine UFO, there was something else that was of interest.

Just like the celluloid newsreel footage of the 1966 Westall Incident, the original photos and negatives had mysteriously disappeared without a trace and, in Roy's case, from nothing less than his personal bank safety deposit box where they had been stored for 20 years.

I only ever had a brief discussion with Mrs Manifold back in 2018, but she had confirmed to me in a phone call that this was in fact correct, that the original photos and negatives had disappeared from the bank's safety deposit box.

Who would have the desire and the means to perform such an undertaking, and why would it have been so important to remove these original photos and negatives from public hands?

Reportedly, neither the DoT nor BASI ever attempted to interview Roy Manifold to do with his having heard an aircraft pass by that evening, nor on the subject of the controversial photographs he had taken.

While the spotlight is set on trying to solve the disappearance of Frederick Valentich, the accent has also swung onto the obvious pattern of a cover-up and covertness associated with all these sightings, Fred's included.

25

Edith

The late Artie Ralston was a licensed aircraft engineer, and so is his son, Andrew, whose maintenance organisation had maintained my company aircraft for many years.

While it has nothing directly to do with the disappearance of Frederick Valentich, it is testimony from a trustworthy source and certain elements are worthy of inclusion.

Edith Ralston's own words are especially relevant in the light of the Westall Incident which took place nearby in 1966.

Of interest are the common elements in these reports, such as the references to the static electricity in the atmosphere and the craft's proximity and effect on the power and the radio stations nearby.

The letter below is her account of what occurred at Hallam, Victoria, around 1962. Hallam is close to Westall in Melbourne's east.

> *Artie Ralston was my boyfriend at the time. He came to pick me up from our basketball dinner in Narre Warren and it was approximately 9 pm on a Saturday night. I don't remember the time of year but I believe it may have been around September.*
>
> *On our way down Hallam Road, we both noticed a row of lights on top of the hill across the valley from my home. Artie asked me if there were any houses on the hill opposite our house, and I replied, "No, the only house that is up there is on the right-hand side of the road and has a large hedge around it so you can't see it."*
>
> *We sat in the car for a few minutes trying to work out what we were observing; this object was so large we had to look left, then right and up*

to see the whole object. We noticed it had large portals running along the length of the craft. As we sat looking at the craft, Artie said that he could see what looked like people standing at the portals.
To me, they looked like shadows.

I had to go down to the house to get a change of clothes to take to Artie's home for the weekend. As I got out of the car, I could feel the static electricity in the night air and the hair on my arms stood up. I very quickly got my clothes and ran back to the car. Artie asked me again what was up on the hill that would have all those lights, and I replied again, "There is nothing up there." At this time, I started to be quite concerned as we had Artie's niece and nephews in the car.
They were so quiet I almost forgot they were there.

At this point in time, Artie started to move the car down the hill and along the valley floor, and as we were driving along, the object moved from the top of the hill and came alongside of us. It didn't come down any lower, it just seemed to be beside us and observing us. We continued up the hill and over the top of the hill, all the time this object was still moving at our rate, which was very slow. We continued over the top of the hill and it was still tracking us. We thought we were tracking it. We continued over Gimpy H'way down another dirt road. I said for us not to go down that road as it was not a through road, but Artie did for about a kilometre, then Artie stopped and got out of the car to observe it a little closer. I told him to get back in the car as we don't know what the heck it was. After a few moments, it just disappeared, away to our left, down Woolamai way. After that, we went straight home to Dandenong, and Artie rang the Herald Sun and told them what we saw. He was told that they were having a lot of reports coming in about the UFO sightings. This craft we saw was huge, massive.

On the Monday morning, on the radio news, a reporter said the radio station at Lyndhurst was completely drained of all its power on the weekend. The power station was at least three kilometres away from the top of the hill where we saw the craft.

To this day, I will never forget this craft and the impact it has had on me and my beliefs about UFOs.

It seems like there is the proclivity for these objects to appear or hover over facilities with great reserves of power, such as electrical power stations and nuclear facilities. It is common that witnesses speak of the energy they feel is given off when in close proximity as has been innocently related in Edith's testimony.

Other well-known compelling reports of UFO visitations include the previously mentioned Westall Incident to the east of Melbourne in 1966, involving 200 schoolchildren and their teachers, as well as the 62 schoolchildren at the Ariel School in Zimbabwe in 1994.

Reports of telepathic communication are not uncommon and so it is perhaps no coincidence that these craft have at times landed at school sites where they possibly detect that among innocent schoolchildren, there are open, uncomplicated minds that will present less barrier to communication.

How do all the witnesses, not just local but worldwide, manage to read from the same hymn book in these encounters, in particular, the Ariel School in Zimbabwe? When called upon, the children all drew the same images of the craft and of its occupants, reporting also a deep and intriguing up-close, one-on-one telepathic experience with the non-humans. So much so that these individuals are still overwhelmed by the experience as adults all these years later.

Here in Australia, the policy of burying information by decision makers in authority is supported by the disappearances of multiple archival records and especially so in the now world-famous Westall case.

So, by design, an ignorance of that evidence and its detail had prevailed among the population at large in the pre-connectivity period that existed when Fred was learning to fly, thereby adding weight to the originality and authenticity of those testimonies.

This is why evidential records from that era are so important. They have more relevance to us today, rather than less.

26

Air Vice-Marshal Alan Reed

Although this testimony regarding the sighting of a UFO is not directly related to the disappearance of Frederick Valentich, I have chosen to include it out of respect for the calibre of the man, the late Air Vice-Marshal Alan Reed. It is also in recognition of his expert witness testimony to do with his own sighting of a UFO and his short but incisive opinion on Valentich.

Aware of my efforts in writing this book, he submitted to me the following account of what, for him, was and has remained something of a mystery encounter many years ago in far north Queensland.

In his own words, the following is a record of a sighting of a UFO that he and a friend had witnessed over Magnetic Island, off the coast of Townsville in the late 1950s.

"... looking towards Magnetic Island, we both saw this cigar-shaped bright light steady then moving very quickly from our right to our left. It was not very high on the horizon, just above Magnetic Island as I recall and appeared to be moving very fast (much quicker than any aircraft of that era) and appeared to stop before disappearing. We actually had it in sight for, I would judge, a couple of minutes. We weren't the only ones who had seen it and a number of people were reported in the Townsville Daily Bulletin as having seen this strange sight.

"I have never been able to explain it. That is the only time I have ever observed anything like it, and it remains in my mind as a UFO. I googled 'Townsville Daily Bulletin UFOs' and while there were a few reports, there were none that I could see going back that far."

And on Valentich:

"It seems the investigation of Valentich's disappearance could certainly have been more thorough, but they probably had a preconceived idea and were not going to challenge that."

Air Vice-Marshal Alan Reed was the last Commanding Officer of Laverton Air Force Base in the west of Melbourne, and I am honoured to have called him and his late son Gus personal friends.

Alan was an accomplished Air Force pilot. He flew F-4 Phantoms when seconded to the USAF, and if there is anyone who would be aware of all the configurations of various aircraft under varying conditions, it would certainly have been Alan Reed.

I had also posed the question whether there are any craft in development, either here in Australia, the USA or even in Russia or China that could perform in the same fashion as the craft that reportedly pursued Frederick Valentich off Cape Otway that evening.

He was candid and adamant, saying that there was absolutely nothing that he was aware of.

Air Vice Marshall Alan Reed passed away on the 24th of July 2021.

27

The Coroner's Report

There wasn't one.

After extensive searches on the internet and through other various channels of enquiry, there were none that I could find.

This was from a handwritten note on a DoT "Minute Paper" related to the comments made by the coroner.

The below was transcribed from the note insofar as it was possible.

DEPARTMENT OF TRANSPORT

MINUTE PAPER

Note:

Following the event of folio 106 [illegible]. Discussed [illegible] matter of Coroner's Inquest with Sgt Bill Kelly of the Coroners Court.

2. He advised:

- *He believed that the police at Apollo Bay would have made out a missing person's report.*
- *The coroner is not interested in holding an inquest into the body.*
- *The coroner has not received a request for an inquest without a body, which can be done under Section 10.*
- *He would not hold an inquest unless the Departmental report indicated some substantial fact indicating a crash and the body was probably dead.*
- *A missing person situation existed at this time.*

- *The Coroner would appreciate a report from DoT for [illegible] holding [illegible] Mr Valentich might ask for an open inquest.*

3. *Passed the above advise onto Mr Woodward [Delegate of the Secretary]. [illegible]*

J.C. Sandercock
ASSU
18/3/82

"J.C. Sandercock" was noted in the DoT report section as the "Assisting Investigator in charge as required".

It is clear that the coroner would not hold an inquest without the lodging of a provision under "Section 10" unless, as stated, a body had been found or there was reason for him to believe that Fred was dead.

No further action was undertaken by the DoT that I could uncover, unless it was actioned subsequent to me writing this book, which is unlikely.

According to Brian, the Acting Sergeant in Charge, to the best of his knowledge, a request for a missing person's report had never been lodged with the Apollo Bay Police.

A missing person's report, at least in those days, had to be as a result of a specific request and to the best of my knowledge, no such request was ever forthcoming, even though there was a realisation and an admission that "a missing person situation existed at the time".

The only detail of any kind that could be located was in the "Department of Transport Aircraft Accident Investigation Summary". It stated in its conclusion in the section titled "Opinion As To Cause": "The reason for the disappearance of the aircraft has not been determined".

Today, at least, if a missing person's report is lodged, it then becomes an ongoing investigation and therefore the case remains open with certain procedures and obligations under the law.

Of interest is the fact that the investigation was based on a missing aircraft and so was managed by the aviation authorities. But there is something of an obvious disconnect, being that police had never been formally engaged in the search for a missing person. What's more, in this instance, the prominent case of a missing person under controversial circumstances.

It is difficult to draw any hard conclusions from all this, but the absence of a missing person's report certainly fits with the whole pattern of what I have determined about this inquiry.

It would be very convenient for certain elements that there was never going to be any ongoing investigation and that, in effect, the matter to do with the case of this missing aviator should remain buried.

Permanently.

28

Brian

The thoughts and angles on Fred's disappearance have come slowly to me and fact gathering has taken many years.

While talking to my friend Brian one day on the phone about an unrelated matter, I just happened to ask him if he would know who the acting policeman in charge of the station at Apollo Bay was when Fred went missing in 1978.

He immediately shot back, "Yes, I do, that was me."

It was one of those moments. A coincidence, and an extraordinary stroke of luck. Not all possible leads were so easy to follow up.

Brian was a police officer stationed at Apollo Bay for 13 years between the years of 1975 to 1988 and was on occasion the Acting Sergeant in Charge at the station.

We talked at length about the investigation, and I asked him if anyone from the DoT or other authorities had contacted him to find out about the missing plane and pilot, and did he know anything more that he could add.

He said, "No, no one apart from Tom Worland from, I think, Channel 9, but I can't be certain."

No authority had ever approached him to ask if he had anything he could contribute in relation to Fred's disappearance.

The television appearance with Tom Worland, public as it was, had not provoked further enquiry from any other authorities.

It should have been an obvious prompt to motivate the investigators, but nothing occurred. Aside from stories about handling the media scrum, he didn't think that he really could contribute anything of value that could help me.

After a little while, he did happen to mention one thing that he thought was curious, passing it on almost as an afterthought.

One morning, about a week or ten days after Fred went missing, he had taken a report in person while on duty at the station regarding the sighting of a body floating in the water on the coast out near Blanket Bay, about 10 kilometres to the southwest along the coast from Apollo Bay.

Two schoolchildren who had been on a school camp at Blanket Bay had been driven to the police station by their teacher to make a report about a body seen floating in the water on the coast. The child who had apparently seen the corpse floating in the sea was hard of hearing and also had a speech disability.

As far as Brian could recall, they would have been about 15 or 16 years of age but unfortunately, he couldn't remember the school.

According to the account, they had been out exploring along the coast, and the child in question had encountered a corpse floating in the water and had reported it to the teacher in attendance, who then drove both the child and his interpreter-friend into the township of Apollo Bay to make the report.

Obviously, no phone service was available in those days and undertaking the drive into the township of Apollo Bay was not an inconsiderable undertaking, being approximately an hour each way on winding dirt roads.

Brian told me that in his earnest opinion, the child had seemed extremely agitated and was communicating by sign language through his friend, a young girl, who acted as interpreter.

He also mentioned that through his own enquiries that the boy was thoroughly reliable, trusted and respected among his school friends and teachers, and that they had all believed his account of what he had seen.

The one thing that threw me off that line of enquiry was that the young schoolboy had also said that the body was dressed in a uniform and that it was similar to a policeman's uniform. All my subsequent enquiries at that time pointed to the fact that Fred was most likely wearing civilian clothes that day, but it seemed that no one knew for sure.

I had also reasoned that even if Fred was wearing the Air Force Air Training Corps uniform, then it couldn't have been him because their uniform was a khaki uniform, so that would have made it incorrect on two counts.

I felt that it was time to let that go and I tried to forget it, but it kept bothering me.

I don't know why I assumed that the Air Force Cadet uniform was khaki at the time, but of course, I was wrong. They were blue, having a light blue shirt and navy pants, just like a policeman's uniform, but the penny didn't drop with me on that point until sometime later. Years later.

Brian had no way of knowing, nor even suspecting, that Fred would have been, could have been, dressed in an Air Force Air Training Corps uniform, similar to a policeman's uniform. I hadn't told him, so the connection was never made.

I had specifically asked that same question to Rhonda, as to what Fred was in fact wearing on the day of his disappearance. She said that Fred would have been in his civilian clothes. But when I pressed her on it and asked her if she had actually seen Fred that day, she replied that she hadn't.

Curiously the investigator's report stated that Rhonda had "seen the car at the airport and that no clothes were in it." But in her 2018 email to me she is very clear that the report was incorrect and that she had not visited the airport to search the vehicle at all, let alone specifically for clothes.

There were too many inconsistencies and errors in the report on Rhonda to cover here.

Quoting from a statement made by Rhonda in her DoT interview report, Fred would have carried with him a "blue short raincoat, very similar to those worn by RAAF personnel, as this was his 'good luck coat', in his words".

It would be reasonable to assume that he was wearing it on the flight that evening over the top of his uniform, predicably casting it off as he entered the water in preparation for the swim to shore.

All things considered, the reported sighting of a body in the water in a uniform was certainly an interesting development, but at the time, I thought that line of inquiry was going nowhere and that it must have been just a tragic coincidence.

But again, Brian confided in me that he had felt strongly that the boy was telling the truth and that there were no other relevant active reports of a missing person that he was aware of.

However, when logically evaluating the veracity of the schoolboy's testimony, how would he come to make up a story of a body, a body in a uniform, and that the uniform was similar to a policeman's uniform no less?

Brian said that prior to driving into Apollo Bay to make the report, the teachers had attended the site and had found no body. It could be argued that this weakens the case for the sighting being verified as true, but in fact, I think that in some ways it strengthens it.

Why would whoever was in charge of the students that day go to all the trouble of driving for at least an hour each way into the township of Apollo Bay on what in those days were substandard dirt roads, if they didn't believe the story had some basis in fact?

More to the point, it also supports Brian's testimony to me of what he had witnessed that day, being that the other schoolchildren and teachers had collectively given that boy a total vote of confidence with respect to his truthfulness and strength of character.

About this, Brian was adamant.

As a footnote to this particular story, Brian had taken the report seriously.

He later attended the scene of the alleged sighting, which was about three or four hundred metres northeast of Blanket Bay, with Inspector Ken Tyler, who had driven down specially from Colac to assist. Colac township is about one hour's drive north of Apollo Bay.

The report was made sometime in the morning, and to the best of Brian's recollection, they had attended onsite around 2 pm.

Blanket Bay isn't far from Cape Otway, with history recording that the supplies for the lightstation had been regularly delivered ashore there by longboat in the 1800s. It was named after the fact that shipwreck survivors often sought shelter there and were given a blanket.

Often, my superficial observation from the air was that the ocean current had appeared to be considerably stronger as I approached Cape Otway from Apollo Bay out to the east, with the westerly flow possibly being influenced by a venturi effect as it rounded Cape Otway. This could have the effect of increasing the speed of the local current up the eastern side, in the local vicinity toward Blanket Bay and is worthy of consideration.

The red arrow marks the location of the Marengo ALA, concealed below a ridge line. The small bay in the foreground is Blanket Bay, about 7 kilometres to the south west of Marengo

They had spent about an hour at the site with Brian, an experienced snorkeler, swimming around in an attempt to locate the corpse, but he had been unsuccessful.

Close, but no cigar.

29

Just one more thing

On good authority, one report from an individual who saw Fred on Saturday the 21st, stated that Fred was definitely wearing his Air Force uniform again on the day he flew down to King Island, same as he had the Wednesday before, which I have verified as being true and correct.

Navy pants, light blue Air Training Corps shirt and polished black shoes.

For reasons known only to himself, the witness then chose to subsequently retract his account of what Fred was wearing that Saturday.

I have to respect that, but let there be no doubt about what I was originally told from a third party who knows the witness well: that Fred was in uniform on the Saturday when he had last seen him, just the same as he had been on the previous Wednesday, but there is still reasonable doubt.

Frustratingly, no headway could subsequently be made with that individual on that front, and to date, other various attempts at obtaining an eyewitness account of what Fred was wearing on his last day have also failed.

In my mind, I am allowing the testimony to stand, albeit qualified, and I am still actively trying to uncover other avenues of inquiry that may shed some further light on that matter.

Darcy Hogan, the Briefing Officer who reportedly processed Fred's flight plan on the afternoon of Saturday 21st unfortunately had no recollection of what Fred had been wearing 47 years ago. It's possible that Fred may have been wearing a pullover at that time and so the uniform might not have been so conspicuous when viewed over the Flight Service briefing office counter.

As already stated in an earlier chapter, Fred had planned to take Rhonda to Squadron Leader Ronald Grandy's home for drinks on the Saturday night after he returned from his flight.

Could Fred have chosen to wear his uniform on the flight that Saturday evening with the intention of wearing it later that night to drinks at Squadron Leader Ronald Grandy's house?

It's not an unreasonable assumption, especially given that he had definitely been wearing it for the previous Wednesday's flight.

Postscript to this story.

Late last night with sleep eluding me, I had watched a YouTube special on Fred's disappearance. This was entirely uncharacteristic and something I have avoided doing to date, preferring instead to develop my own thoughts on the mystery.

The program entitled 'The Unexplained Disappearance of Australian Pilot Frederick Valentich' runs for about fifty-six and a half minutes. After having watched it, I immediately emailed the publisher with instructions to "stop the press", as the book wasn't far off going to print.

There wasn't anything especially remarkable or revealing in the body of the documentary, which appears to have been made not long after Fred's disappearance. Nonetheless, I felt committed to watching it all the way through as it contained a reasonable amount of footage of a young Steve Robey and of Fred's father, Guido, a distinguished gentleman of northern Italian heritage.

Towards the end of the short documentary was a re-enacted scene set at the breakfast table at the Valentich household on the morning of Fred's disappearance.

This scene was narrated by Guido himself, saying that he will never forget that morning. He spoke of how Fred was cheerful and in in good spirits that day and then he added with a certain sadness, that this was the last time he ever had contact with his son.

Given the sentimental circumstances surrounding the reason for its creation, it would be reasonable to assume that under Guido's critical eye, the context of that re-enactment, brief as it was, would have been factually correct in every respect.

Significantly, the actor portraying Fred in the re-enactment was wearing an Airforce uniform, a blue shirt with epaulettes "just like a policeman's uniform", and it would also be fair to assume that this had been as a result of information provided firsthand by Guido himself.

Late as it is, this is a vital revelation and perhaps the strongest indication to date that Fred had been wearing his Airforce Training Corps uniform on the day of his disappearance.

All of this taken collectively, adds considerable weight to the story of a body in uniform floating in the water just north of Blanket Bay.

30

The ATSB and NASA

My email to both the ATSB and NASA, dated 24th of September 2018.

To whom it may concern,

I have important and relevant information with respect to the unsolved disappearance of pilot, Frederick Valentich in a Cessna 182 at around last light on the evening of 21st of October 1978.

I have interviewed a local Apollo Bay resident that swears he saw the aircraft on descent in and east or S/E direction off Elliot river in the vicinity of Apollo Bay while driving down the Barham River road ie returning approximately eastward to Apollo Bay. I drove him out to the location and he recreated the event onsite with me.

He said his attention was first drawn to the aircraft by his niece who was present in the vehicle with him.

In a general recollection of events, according to his testimony, he saw nothing at first glance (looking out to his right) then looked again and saw the aircraft and said "that's an aeroplane" to which his niece replied "Yes I can see that but what's the bright light above it".

He looked back and said he saw a fast moving bright light which came and went and which then followed the aircraft as it descended out of sight below the hills toward the sea.

The aircraft had its lights on and from what I can determine the aircraft was returning from Cape Otway toward the township and that this time frame was after the recorded conversation with Flight Service and right on last light. Questioning him closely he said the aircraft was definitely upright and level but in a descent with this bright object following right behind and on descent as well.

He's a credible witness and I have no reason not to believe him.

If this report is true, and I believe that it is, then it changes the whole outcome of the history of events on the day.

As I have always suspected, the pilot did not suffer from spatial disorientation (it was a blue bird evening by all accounts) nor was he on a mission of self-harm as was often alluded to in the months that followed.

If this report is true then the investigation should be re-opened without delay as my witness is not getting any younger.

It is imperative that this young man's name is cleared.

Just for your further information, so convinced am I by the genuineness of this witness that I have also put a report into the FAA who hold an open file on the matter.

It is my belief that the aircraft lies in shallow water possibly not that far out from Apollo Bay.

As a footnote let me add that he (my witness) went to ground with the information because the locals, including the local police, said that he'd been drinking and that he was seeing things. He was offended naturally by this and I believe him when he says hadn't been drinking on the night, nor is he a drinker as such to this day.

Also for the record he was returning from a rabbiting excursion with his two sons and two nieces in the back of the vehicle.

They were all quite young and he is not at all sure if they would remember the course of events accurately at all.

He also said although he became friends with the pilots father Guido Valentich, now passed on, non of the authorities, ether DoT or BASI ever made an attempt to interview him as neither did they make any attempt to interview Roy Manifold and his wife who were in their hut at Crayfish Bay, down near Cape Otway and heard the aircraft pass by.

Victor F. Bongiorno
Chief Pilot / Owner
Apollo Bay Aviation
(Bush Pilots Australia Pty. Ltd.)

The response from the Air Transport Safety Bureau (ATSB).

Dear Mr Bongiorno,

Thank you for your email. I have consulted with my manager and can advise that the ATSB will not investigate this accident any further. The principal reason for this decision is that, as the investigation was finalised in 1982 by the then-Department of Transport, the passage of time means that any recollections could not be relied upon and there is no means to independently verify any witness accounts.

Additionally, the ATSB's primary focus is on enhancing safety with respect to fare-paying passengers, and in particular, those transport safety matters that may present a significant threat to public safety and are the subject of widespread public interest. Our resourcing and our mission means that we must be strategic, investigating those incidents and accidents that are likely to be of the greatest benefit to the broader transport industry, and which have the greatest potential of identifying systemic issues in aviation, marine and rail transport operations.

Acknowledging your motivation to further investigate this occurrence, there is limited safety benefit to the travelling public in pursuing this matter.

Regards,

While there are no plans to re-open the investigation it must be remembered that a young man has lost his life in mysterious circumstances and that it remains one of Australia's prominant unsolved aviation mysteries.

The following is NASA's response that was delivered in hardcopy to my Marengo address.

Response Letters from NASA.

In reading the responses from the two authorities, it is impossible not to be impressed with the level of attention and recognition that NASA affords to witnesses with respect to UFO sightings, not just in their own backyard or their own country, but worldwide.

NASA's modus operandi is to collect and collate information regardless of historical time constraints and geographical boundaries.

The ATSB's response to me was both excluding and immutable, stating that they will not re-open the case, which is curious given the new information available and the obviously inadequate response during the original investigation.

It would be quite fair to say that there is a stark difference in the response between the ATSB and NASA and that the comparison between the two authorities is as obvious as night and day.

Thanks to public media, there is more knowledge and acceptance of these sightings among the general public today than there was all those years ago. The release of this information is timely for the sake of Fred's memory and because the evidence contained herein is in itself well above being wholly circumstantial, there is justifiable cause to re-examine the DoT's open finding in this case as exemplified by the following transcripts.

31

The power of circumstantial evidence

Quotes from the 2023 trial and cold case conviction of 74-year-old former New South Wales schoolteacher Chris Dawson for the murder of his wife Lynnette in 1982.

Justice Ian Harrison [*presiding*] and the use of *wholly* circumstantial evidence and the role it played in the 2022 conviction.

"The case against Mr Dawson is wholly circumstantial …," said Justice Ian Harrison.

And further, from Justice Ian Harrison … "but when regard is had to their combined force, I am left in no doubt!"

"… as soon as there is doubt, the accused is given the benefit of that doubt, but for Justice Harrison, circumstances were enough."

"… forty years had passed, and the judge must base his verdict wholly upon circumstantial evidence alone. Legal experts say the case was unusual due to its lack of physical evidence, no body, no weapon, no forensic evidence and there was no direct evidence."

"The CSI effect (Crime Scene Investigations effect) typically said forensic evidence becomes far more conclusive, but it wasn't a slur on the justice system to describe a case as being only circumstantial. Circumstantial evidence can be extremely damning if all the circumstances line up… and that's what Justice Harrison said it did in this case."…Rick Sarre, Emeritus Professor of Law and Criminal Justice at The University of South Australia.

Source: *ABC News*, Sydney.

At the risk of appearing dramatic, the use of the comparison of a recent murder conviction is, I feel, appropriate and justified.

The comparisons are simple and obvious.

There is no physical evidence and a long time period has elapsed with the eventual finding handed down being based solely on circumstantial evidence.

What the other craft actually was is unknown but given numerous other sightings and accounts of a strange light in the sky that evening, it is enough evidence for me to conclude beyond reasonable doubt that Fred had been telling the truth that evening when he reported a UFO, and that it was also reason enough for him to have taken the appropriate evasive action in an attempt to throw his pursuer off his tail.

Collectively the weight of the evidence contained in this book is enough justification for re-opening the investigation into Fred's disappearance hopefully at the end of this long day giving some closure to his surviving family and to Rhonda.

Any external and unknown influence that has precipitated the loss of an aircraft and its occupant is a matter of air safety and so, contrary to the ATSB's assertion in their email response to me, not only do I think that it's an ongoing matter of air safety but that it has considerable historical significance to the Australian aviation sector and therefore warrants re-investigation.

32

The final minutes

Old charts are timeless in a way screens never can be.

The aviation advisory for aircraft navigating Bass Strait stated that "Bass Strait crossings" are to be flown at a minimum of 2,000 feet above mean sea level (AMSL) to ensure radio contact with Melbourne Flight Service, and Fred's flight plan nominated that he was maintaining a general cruising altitude of below 5,000 feet ("BO50").

That designation is available because it allows the pilot to vary cruising altitudes at will to avoid any weather, terrain or other aircraft.

More specifically, Fred had stated both on his flight plan and clearly on the radio during the course of the flight that he was maintaining 4,500 feet above mean sea level on his south-southeast leg to King Island.

It has been documented worldwide that during various encounters with UFOs, radio communications have been lost and that internal reciprocating combustion engines have lost power, either partially or completely, as a result of interference with the aircraft's electrical ignition system.

During the final six-minute radio transmission with Melbourne Flight Service, Fred had clearly and calmly relayed his cruise power setting for the leg south across Bass Strait as "23/24" and clearly confirmed his cruising altitude as "Four and a half thousand, Four Five Zero Zero" (4,500 feet), but at that point he had also reported that he was experiencing engine problems.

I choose to take Fred entirely at his word when he reported to Melbourne Flight Service in his status report that his engine was running rough – "the engine is rough idling, I've got it set to 23/24 and the thing is coughing" – and that it would be highly unlikely that any rough running was coincidentally due to conventional mechanical or fuel-related problems.

Whether this effect would have been intentional on the part of the visitor or whether it was a matter of circumstance is impossible to determine.

Other encounters where UFOs have hovered over or around nuclear missile silos state that nuclear warheads in both the US and Russia have unexpectedly gone into various stages of alert, or that power stations have seemingly been drained of power while the craft was in the vicinity.

References to documented encounters are plentiful and verifiable. To my knowledge, they have occurred in Australia, the US and Russia, among other places.

It seems logical that Fred, alone and threatened with the pressure of an unknown craft in his direct vicinity, would have done what any pilot who was trying to maintain control of both his aircraft and of his destiny would do: depart his flight planned track to King Island at his earliest convenience contrary to his very recent statement to Melbourne Flight Service stating his intentions were to "go to King Island".

Things change quickly and he would have been re-assessing his options as they arose in the rapidly changing scenario. For him, a rough-running engine and impending last light would have suddenly become major, major considerations.

In a desperate effort to escape from whatever was pursuing him, the easiest course of action would be to divert and descend into the little bush strip that he knew existed at Marengo, Apollo Bay, where he would at least have a chance to get on the ground and re-consider his options.

Given that at 4,500 feet (cruising altitude) and that the glide ratio for a Cessna 182 is 9.3:1, that would theoretically allow a distance of nearly 13 kilometres (just under 7 nautical miles) that could be covered in a glide, dead stick (ie, engine out) and nil wind. That would assume adopting the optimum glide speed of 68 knots for that aircraft, weight-dependent, but call it that.

In any event, on it's own it would have been far too slow for him to have made it back where he was seen over the Marengo hills by last light. Consider also the negative effects a 15-knot headwind component would have had on reducing his effective ground speed and glide distance on that return leg.

Fred would have had to descend at a much higher speed than an effective groundspeed of just 53 knots (68 knots minus the 15 knots headwind component) in an attempt to locate the landing area with whatever light left was left; seconds mattered, and he was out of time.

Without the luxury of radar coverage, it is impossible to accurately determine Fred's track or give a precise location for where he would have made his decision to divert.

The point of all this is to demonstrate that, given the quite reasonable assumption he would have been further than 7 nautical miles from Apollo Bay at his decision point, it would be reasonable to assume that he had the benefit of partial engine power, or at least enough to manoeuvre.

Fred had approximately six minutes of light left between his last transmission at 19:12 local time and Official Last Light at 19:18 EST to divert and find the airstrip and get his aircraft on the ground. Given his lack of local knowledge, this would have been a very challenging undertaking and accent is being placed on anything that may have allowed Fred to realistically accomplish this.

At 19:10, he reported that he was (already) orbiting, and a lot would depend on at what point prior along his original flight planned track he had made the deliberate and reactive decision to orbit, and also as to the direction and size of that orbit.

He may well have been factoring all that in from the outset when he had begun to orbit and, in any event, it makes sense that he would have instinctively favoured the pilot's side of the aircraft when choosing a direction to orbit and so he would have made a left-hand orbit. When on a south-south easterly heading, this manoeuvre would have helped in positioned him just that much closer to Apollo Bay.

What should also be considered is that he had 4,500 feet to lose in a few minutes and on the assumption that he had an engine that was only partially capable of delivering normal power, it was a bonus. A big one.

This means that he could potentially have utilised that height above the airfield and turned it into speed as much as possible while recognising the structural limitation on the airframe. This number is measured in knots and is known as the aircraft's Never Exceed Speed or "Vne".

This limitation is clearly given as a number in the aircraft's flight manual and is also marked as a red line on the aircraft's Air Speed Indicator (ASI). To the best of my knowledge, in that aircraft, it is 172 knots or approximately 320 kilometres per hour. Speeds in excess of this risk structural damage to the airframe.

Bringing these factors together, such as the aircraft's Vne of 172 knots, the prevailing headwind of 15 knots on that return leg into Apollo Bay, at best Fred would have had a groundspeed of around 160 knots unless he had pushed the aircraft's speed past Vne.

I think Fred would have used up every bit of this speed advantage and maybe more, lowering the little aircraft's nose in a non-typical, desperate manoeuvre in an attempt to save seconds. Priority one was to locate the little coastal airstrip that he knew existed back at Apollo Bay using the last few precious minutes of light that remained.

So in the 6 minutes between his last transmission at 1912 and Last Light when Fred was sighted by Merv on descent off the Elliot River and working on an effective groundspeed of close to 160 knots, Fred could have been up to 16 nautical miles off Marengo at the point of his diversion. This affords a practical perspective to the whole timeline.

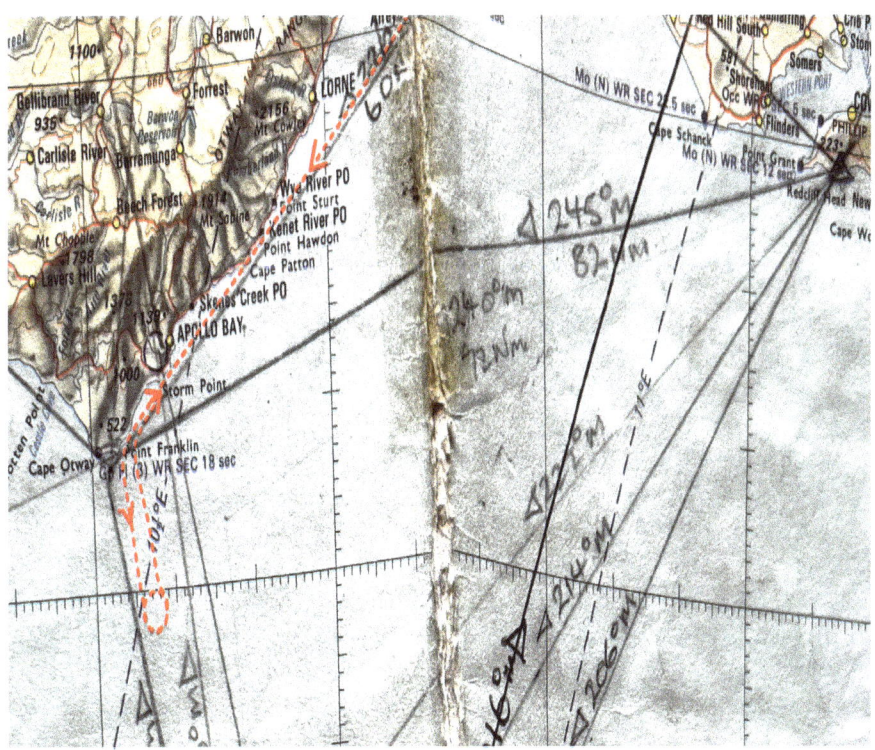

A simulated reconstruction of Fred's track

All these things add weight to the credibility of Merv O'Meara's testimony, not so much that they are required to confirm the veracity of his testimony, but more that they don't at all preclude that testimony by making it impossible for Fred to have been able to have made it back to the airfield area in accordance with the timeline.

Considering the pressure that had suddenly and unexpectedly come to bear on him and taking into account all the available evidence given in Merv's testimony, when he found himself unable to locate the airstrip and with darkness upon him, he would have then been left with three options:

1. Climb back up to lowest safe altitude and proceed to King Island as originally planned, which would have been very unlikely as it would have meant a Bass Strait crossing with what seemed to be a hostile craft in close proximity.

2. Climb back up to lowest safe altitude and divert back to Moorabbin, which again didn't solve the problem he had with whatever it was that was taking so much interest in him and his aircraft.

3. Ditch in the dark as close to the coast as possible where he would at least have had half a chance to make it ashore.

This last remaining unattractive option, hopefully being a controlled water landing, into the cold dark ocean would have been mentally challenging to say the least, and I feel Fred would have delayed that decision for as long as he possibly could. Perhaps even until it was unavoidable.

A ditching at night would have been a demanding manoeuvre given it would probably be almost impossible to accurately judge the last few feet of descent and to slow the aircraft's speed by conducting a "flare" onto the surface of the water in the dark.

Fred feared the water because he couldn't swim, and understandably, that fear would have elevated as he made his final descent knowing he was committed to a ditching.

My understanding was that, at best, he could manage in the water was a dogpaddle, but whichever way he looked at it that night, it would have been clear to him that finally, for him, "the sky above was of absolutely no use" and that he was indeed out of options.

Merv O'Meara's account is vital in all of this and when connecting the dots with Brian's testimony, it is reasonable to arrive at a conclusion as to the final resting place for Frederick Valentich's Cessna aircraft, VH-DSJ: somewhere in the Bass Strait between Cape Otway and Apollo Bay and most likely in the vicinity of Blanket Bay.

This is where the long trail has led me. This is where I think Fred had found himself and it is what I think actually did take place that night.

Otherwise, why didn't Fred simply exercise the privilege of his night rating and climb up and fly back to safety, landing at Moorabbin Airport or even to continue to King Island?

Answer: because he couldn't. Stands to reason. Because he couldn't.

It's very simple, he would have if he could have, but only having partial engine power meant that option was no longer available to him.

It all says to me that he still had company in the very real form of a UFO, and as such, with compromised engine performance would have been unable to achieve climb power, and this would have been a major factor in any of his decision-making.

Even if full engine power had been restored, would the UFO return and the problem suddenly re-occur when he was halfway across Bass Strait in the dark?

Excluding the effects of hypothermia, controlled water landings in light planes, even a fixed-gear light plane such as the one Fred was flying, typically have a high degree of survivability. It is impossible to know if Fred was aware of this, and if this had formed part of his decision-making on the night.

In a controlled emergency water landing, the aircraft's protruding fixed landing gear would contact the water first, and predictably, the aircraft would have flipped onto its roof and settled upside down on the water.

While this sounds like the worst of options, it could be argued that it wasn't.

Providing Fred's seat belt was snug and secure, it would have held him in the seat after the landing. Providing he could free himself and exit the aircraft, he would have had the advantage of the inverted and partially submerged airframe of the high-wing Cessna as a raft for a short period to enable him to gather his strength and his courage for the swim to shore, such as it would be.

In reality, it would have been a demanding swim even for the most accomplished of swimmers at night in that frigid water.

Given that in that final minute or two, while he was committed to ditching, Fred would have been probably unable to judge his distance from the coast in the dark and therefore would have had to be conservative in his judgement of where he planned to touchdown on the water in case he overshot the landing and hit the rocks.

It wouldn't be something that could be easily altered at the last minute unless he turned the aircraft away and that may have put him further from land than he could have afforded.

Not being a capable swimmer was a critical limitation.

Ideally, he would have had to judge the distance in the darkness as he manoeuvred his lame aircraft toward the coast in preparation for the ditching, as that was the "into wind" direction considering the effects that a forecast 15-knot north-westerly wind would have. This is absolutely critical to observe in circumstances such as a forced landing on land or at sea and would have been prominent in his reasoning at that time.

The simple maths are that if you get it wrong and land downwind (as opposed to landing into a headwind), then the touchdown speed would be increased by twice the headwind component, being another (2 × 15) 30 knots or an extra 56 kilometres per hour higher than that of a landing executed into wind.

The effective touchdown speed on the water, if he got it right, would have been a survivable 45 knots (83 kilometres per hour), or if he got it wrong, 75 knots (139 kilometres per hour), immeasurably increasing the risk of the forced landing not being survivable.

It is evident that judging the wind correctly would be a critical factor, given his lack of prowess in the water.

This was all to be executed in the dark so that the aircraft would wind up ditching as close to the land mass as possible to give himself half a chance of getting ashore, all with little or no height or distance perception. A terrifying proposition.

It was marked on the flight plan that Fred had at least one lifejacket onboard, but if the report of the body on the rocks is to be given any credibility, and I do give it credibility, then he wasn't wearing one.

The official report into Fred's disappearance is full of errors and untruths. One statement that is untrue is that Rhonda stated that, in her opinion, Fred would have "entered the aircraft wearing a lifejacket". Rhonda refutes this.

Her statement to me in a 2018 email was, "He never entered any aeroplane with a lifejacket on." This information is of great importance. Not only does it yet again call into question the accuracy of the official report and the motivation and competency of the investigators, but it also helps to confirm my assertion that he wasn't wearing a lifejacket the evening he departed Moorabbin Airport.

While it was mandatory to carry a lifejacket, it wasn't mandatory to actually don the lifejacket outside of gliding distance to land when flying over water at or above 2,000 feet above mean sea level.

As stated, Fred's cruising level across Bass Strait on that evening was 4,500 feet, and all this also gives me reason to believe that he wasn't wearing his lifejacket in the aircraft that evening.

With the benefit of an older head, I always donned my lifejacket when crossing Bass Strait, no matter what the flight planned level, because I knew from hard experience how difficult it is to put on a lifejacket mid flight during controlled flight without the benefit of the use of an autopilot, let alone in an emergency situation like the one Fred had found himself in.

Early in my flying days in the early 1980s, I observed it was commonplace for pilots to elect not to actually wear lifejackets during Bass Strait crossings regardless of level, for whatever reason. Perhaps it was pride, perhaps it was that they felt like they were being overcautious and tempting fate, I don't know, but that was definitely my observation of how it was back in the day.

The mentality of safety wasn't enforced then as it is today, with the fitting of seatbelts in new cars being mandated in 1972 but the wearing of which remained unenforced here in Victoria until the early 1980s.

In the chaos of a ditched and upturned aircraft in the dark, there is every reason to assume that he had become separated from this vital piece of equipment, leaving it behind in the submerging aircraft.

All of these things considered, it would be fair to assume that if Fred was not wearing his lifejacket when he became airborne out of Moorabbin earlier that day, then he did not have it on when things started to happen that evening at 19:06 AEST off the coast at Cape Otway, by which time it would have been too late. The die had been cast.

In the sequence of events, the decision not to don the lifejacket when departing Moorabbin earlier that evening was possibly the most unfortunate single event to have occurred that day.

A lifejacket can save the life of even a poor swimmer but this night, his lifejacket was of absolutely no use to him.

He would have been far too busy to then have undertaken that action in the following final desperate minutes: reaching behind for his lifejacket, releasing his seat belt, taking his hands off the controls of a potentially over-speeding aircraft in the dark, leaning forward and donning and fastening the tapes of the lifejacket (more than likely tie-on tapes in those days) and then re-securing and tightening his seatbelt in anticipation of the inevitable mass deceleration that was about to occur.

All this when he was so pre-occupied with what was happening both inside and outside the aircraft, that being the proximity of the other craft, attempting to broadcast on the radio, controlling the aircraft and maintaining a proper instrument scan to enable him to keep the wings level in the rapidly decreasing low light conditions.

As he approached a darkening coastline, he would have been still looking for what might be the airstrip, ensuring he didn't overspeed, monitoring his decreasing altitude and trying not to make contact with the surface of the water early and unexpectedly.

If the UFO was still in close proximity, and according to Merv's witness statement it was, quite possibly the aircraft's electrical system was compromised, not only the radio but any electronics, including the all-important instrument panel lights.

From personal experience, losing instrument panel lighting in the inky darkness over Bass Strait at night is bad enough at cruising altitude, but it would have been terrifying for a low-hour pilot in a low-level emergency situation.

The flight plan wasn't correct when it stated that the aircraft was fitted with a survival beacon which, if fitted, would have activated on impact with the water, sending out a signal to assist search-and-rescue aircraft while it was still afloat; this is on the proviso that the signal had not been attenuated by the proximity of the UFO.

I have it on good authority that it wasn't fitted with a survival beacon even though it sported the short survival beacon antennae at the rear of the fuselage.

If I am correct, given the timeline of events, a few things would have taken place in a very short period of time.

Firstly, as a result of interference most likely caused by another craft jamming his transmissions and then as he descended, due to topographical limitations, Fred would have lost any chance of any further radio communication with Melbourne Flight Service and the steadying voice of Flight Service Officer Steve Robey, forever.

Radio communications then weren't as good as they are today. In that specific location, any VHF radio broadcasts, which are predominantly line of sight, would very likely have been attenuated by the high ground of the Otway coast, depending upon his altitude and his location south of the mainland out in Bass Strait.

In any event, his last recognised transmission was at 19:12:28 AEST (local time), which was then followed by 17 seconds of "attenuated" radio signal.

The "17 seconds" has been the subject of much analysis, speculation and controversy.

In the absence of any information to the contrary, I'm of the opinion that the controversial 17-second period at the end of the six-minute transmission was a fully jammed or attenuated radio signal and any suggestion that it was metal scraping upon metal, which is a widely lauded opinion, doesn't sound feasible, nor does it even sound at all possible.

If it were in fact metal on metal, then it would imply that something quite irregular was taking place and at that time, the mic was "open" and transmitting during that event.

If that were the case, it would also stand to reason that the transmission being received by Melbourne would have been interspersed with the sound of the pilot's voice combined with any other background noise, such as the alleged scraping metal as the pilot had attempted to re-establish contact with the mic button depressed. Otherwise, how else would such a transmission have been made?

But none of this was apparent.

More to the point, if Fred had choreographed his own disappearance, how could he have so expertly manufactured and executed the delivery of the last 17 seconds of "open mic" at the end of his transmission, so much so that no one, including NASA, have ever been able to provide a logical explanation as to the origin or the reason for its existence?

This must go a long way to support the argument that the recording is genuine in every way and that the pilot was telling it as he saw it during that final exchange, and that it was not an attempt by an individual to attract sympathy and notoriety in his final moments.

The investigator's note on Rhonda's interview incorrectly stated that "she was of the opinion the 'metallic noise' mentioned in the newspaper could have been the seat sliding rearward". This seems an amateurish observation at best and is yet another example of that report's lack of detail and factual incorrectness.

More to the point, Rhonda refutes this version of events in the official file report in her 2018 email to me: "I hadn't heard the tape, and I don't think I knew about the noise at that time. Maybe I might have read about the noise, but I hadn't been told any information about that noise."

Secondly, he would have descended to below what would have been his lowest safe altitude (4,000 feet AMSL on that leg according to Fred's flight plan), which in broad terms is a cruising altitude 1,000 feet above the highest point of land within 10 nautical miles of his aircraft's position.

This was soon to become a critical consideration for him as the minutes passed and he entered official darkness at precisely 19:18 AEST. His last communication with Melbourne Flight Service had ended at around 19:12, six minutes prior to official last light.

Thirdly, after having departed from his official flight plan in an attempt to escape his pursuer, he was then committed to either locate and land at the Marengo airstrip or to execute an emergency landing on water, a ditching at night, with "committed" then being the operative word. He was out of options.

The Marengo Authorised Landing Area (ALA) was only a grass clearing between the trees back in those days and lay 2 kilometres just to the south of the main township of Apollo Bay.

It runs in an east-west direction and was located right on the coast. It was short enough at 750 metres effective length, 2% uphill to the west and at that time it still had power lines across the eastern threshold. These reduced the effective landing distance when landing from the east, the direction from which Fred would have been approaching and stood ready to snare an unwary pilot in the looming darkness. These together with high ground rising to 800-

feet off the western end created a challenging environment for young Fred when attempting to get his aircraft on the ground in the fading light.

High ground off the western end of the runway presents a threatening environment in the fading ligh

An elevated view of Marengo ALA in 2022, barely identifiable in daylight as a green line across the foreground. Far more visible than it would have been in 1978

The landing area is also concealed by a ridgeline along the southern side, the side from which Fred would have been approaching the field in the half-light, and it was a lot less distinguishable in 1978 than it is today in 2025 as a sealed defined airstrip.

Originally established by the local doctor Dr Ralph Capponi in the 1960s, it had been shaped out of the scrub, rough and ready. Dr Capponi was known for taxiing his aircraft two kilometres into town along an often-empty Great Ocean Road to fill up with fuel at the local bowser, occasionally running afoul of the local policeman, Senior Constable Sexton, who had booked him for doing it.

Besides being a colourful piece of history, the relevance of mentioning this is that it is an example of just how remote the area had been, not so very long prior in the 1960s.

Things hadn't changed that much by October 1978, and it is very conceivable that few people were in the area to witness the events as they had unfolded that evening.

On occasions, when transiting at altitude, I had observed the small ALA as I passed by on crayfish runs to King Island in the 1980s. In anything like poor light conditions, it was very hard to identify. This would have been a lot harder at low level which is where Fred most likely would have found himself on that evening. As I have already explained, things happen quickly when at low level in an aircraft, and especially in low-light conditions.

Generally, I found the easiest way to identify the strip as I passed was to look for the white cross on the ground in among the trees if it was out, which indicated that the landing area was closed, most likely due to the soft surface as it was in a very high rainfall area.

This was the easiest way. Otherwise, it was a difficult landing strip to identify.

Although the Cessna 182 is a very good bush aircraft able to handle rough short strips, it is fairly certain that Fred did not have an in-depth knowledge of the area or of that airstrip's location. Without being previously "checked into" that strip, it would have been extremely challenging for a low-hour pilot to locate and execute a safe landing right on last light.

In that unfamiliar environment and the lee of the Otway Ranges with a darkening sea rising to meet him, there is no doubt Fred would have been feeling the pressure, all with the threat of a pursuing UFO which he would have been doing his very best to be rid of.

I am of the considered opinion that this was the position that Fred had found himself in and so was committed to ditching within a few kilometres, somewhere west of the Marengo airstrip back towards or just west of Blanket Bay, probably a couple of minutes flight time in that aircraft.

Overflying the coast in an attempt to locate the airstrip and flying westward up the valley in close proximity to those hills with darkness falling is an unpleasant, intimidating experience, even for someone who knows what they are doing.

It would be a very good reason for a low-hour pilot, unfamiliar with the local geography, not to cross the coast at low level to look for the landing area in the dark.

A seat-of-the-pants sense of self-preservation would not have allowed Fred to venture into that place with high ground looming in the darkness in an effort to locate the airstrip. It would have been foolhardy for him to have done so, and I'm of the opinion he elected to take what mustn't have been an attractive option either, being the lesser of two evils: to continue towards Cape Otway in the assumption that he could again make a turn back east with the intention to ditch near the harbour or on Marengo beach.

By the time his aircraft was identified over the top of the Marengo hills by Merv and his niece, he was on a steep descent out over the water, with a UFO close behind and darkness rapidly falling.

It should be emphasised that both craft were on a steep descent heading approximately east at that time, which is in the opposite direction to Blanket Bay where the reported sighting of the body in the water had occurred. How far he continued eastward past

Marengo isn't known, but I would say not far, given the pressure of time.

It is hard to determine why Fred would have then elected to fly back away from the beach and past the lights of the little township of Marengo to wind up ditching his aircraft in an isolated location in the darkness, and I have spent some time pondering that question.

It could be simply that at that time he still wasn't mentally committed to ditching the aircraft and to avoid the water while there was any chance at all of effecting a conventional landing. Instead, he was still focused on finding where the little airstrip lay, taking a decision to circle back to make one last pass in a desperate effort to do so.

At that point, the little landing area would have been right under his nose.

But tragically, just like in Hemingway's old man of the sea, Fred had gone out too far. A simple truth. He had gone out too far.

A few minutes earlier would've seen him on the ground safe, able to speak of his encounter, relegated then to the long line of story tellers and dreamers. Just another eyewitness to something so amazing.

But that wasn't to be, and while for me at least he has ultimately attained believability, it has come at a high price.

If he had known just enough in the half-light to keep the Henty Reef under his left wing in the decending turn, and with flaps and landing lights effectivly disabled, taken up a westerly heading, deftly sideslipping the little aircraft in the descent, the small landing area would have eventually become obvious.

Eventually the trees and the grass would have come into focus, and slowly, raising the nose of the aeroplane, he would have felt the wheels make contact with dear mother earth, rolling confidently along on solid ground.

But he didn't know. How could he have known? It takes years to acquire that kind of confidence, and at that point Fred was completely alone, with only God to hold his hand.

So close, and yet so far.

From my recollection it was just a clearing in the coastal scrub. Far less distinguishable in the half light than it is as a sealed runway today

Missing it, he turned back into the southwest towards Blanket Bay and the Parker River at low level, now probably in complete darkness in a compromised position and still with the UFO in close company and an engine delivering partial power.

For Fred, things would have compounded rapidly and unexpectedly over the course of a few minutes and it would have been difficult for a new pilot, any pilot, to accept that all options had been finally exhausted and to come to grips with the massive mental undertaking of making the command decision to ditch the aircraft in a controlled manner onto a cold dark ocean knowing he couldn't swim.

At this point, he would have decided to either not try and turn back towards the township at low level or, possibly, had tried to turn back northeastwards towards the township in the darkness and in doing so had contacted the water during that manoeuvre, but this is now total conjecture.

Or, was it just that he was simply unable to maintain height any longer and fearful of making a turn and losing control, and so was compelled to settle his aircraft on the water as best he could, because he had no choice?

Executing a low-level turn close to the water in limited visibility in a high-wing aircraft like the Cessna 182, where the horizon you are turning towards becomes obscured by the lowered wing, would have been demanding in the extreme in daylight.

For him, a low-hour pilot, such a turn at night close to the surface of the water and without reference to lights or the horizon with compromised engine power and electrical system it would have been an impossible, terrifying manoeuvre.

Passing Marengo, Fred could have made the initial turn southwestward back toward the airstrip's location while there was just enough light left and while he still had the lights of the little town in sight for visual reference.

He probably wouldn't quite have had the experience to realise that in this last desperate attempt to locate a landing area, he was sealing his fate by turning back into the Bass Strait darkness, past where he thought the little airstrip may lie. It was an impossible situation, where the night sky, the sea and the rocky headlands would soon all become as one.

Looking west just prior to last light in exactly the same meteorological conditions that Fred would have encountered. "A clear night with light mid-level cloud.

In this scenario, spatial disorientation was a distinct possibility and the margin for error is nil.

Common sense would dictate to him that he should avoid travelling too far out to sea in the dark and would have probably ditched in the ocean as close as he dared to the rocky coast. Given the effects of the prevailing current, it is reasonable to assume that he had wound up ditching somewhere southwest of Blanket Bay, where his body was eventually sighted floating near the rocks by the young schoolboy.

The 1968 Cessna aircraft was fitted with bladder tanks that would have been less likely to rupture in a forced landing than the later model "wet wing" aluminium fuel tanks. As such, they could have provided at least some buoyancy after a controlled landing on water, given that the tanks were nearly full. This is all in the assumption that Fred was successful in that manoeuvre.

It is a distinct possibility as nothing at all has ever been found washed up of the Cessna after all these years; no plastics, no lifejackets, no seats and no tell-tale fuel slick on the surface of the water, nothing that would indicate a catastrophic impact with the water had taken place and so the case for a controlled landing having occurred is strengthened.

The specific gravity of Aviation Gasoline (Avgas) is 0.71 of water and less in saltwater which may, to some degree, have slowed the aircraft's submersion and descent to the seabed, allowing it to drift with the current from the site of the ditching.

In a simple calculation, after deducting 50 litres of flight fuel from the aircraft's tanks, there would have been up to 270 litres of aviation gasoline remaining onboard. This would have afforded it some extra flotation as it drifted on a northeasterly trajectory prior to settling on the seabed.

Although this would probably have been of minimal assistance to Fred on the night, it may be important information to factor into any future search for the wreck's location.

Studies of local ocean currents were undertaken in the 1980s by the Geelong Port Authority in an effort to find a solution to the harbour mouth at Apollo Bay silting up. These revealed that the ocean currents in the vicinity of Cape Otway move at an average of 4 knots northeast along the coast back up toward Melbourne.

Retired Apollo Bay cray fisherman, Nick Polgeest, told me that he had always searched to the east for craypots along that coast that had drifted from where they had been "set".

Never west.

33

The last word

As I proceeded to write this book, my eyes have been opened to the pattern of events associated with not only this case but also of many other UFO sightings and encounters which have occurred on our own home soil.

Over the last 20 years, something else has been revealed as I made routine enquiries surrounding the events of Fred's disappearance.

At the outset, my mind was more or less focused on the events specifically surrounding the disappearance of Frederick Valentich. But as I progressed, wilful cover-up and distortion of relevant facts by the investigators associated with this and other UFO cases has become apparent.

Unwilling at first to give myself the benefit of the doubt with respect to the results of my findings, I first conceded that I was perhaps being overly creative with my assumptions and conclusions.

Now, not only am I convinced that Fred was being pursued by a UFO, but it has become obvious there has been another enemy in our midst hiding in plain sight, with the lines of engagement having been purposefully blurred by a sleight of hand.

I am the one who feels like I have been abducted by the cult and who has been made to drink the Kool-Aid as I attempted to determine what is smoke and what is fact, what is the truth and who is spinning the false narratives?

This time, instead of the conspiracy theorists, it is the general population who have been unknowingly tricked into drinking the Kool-Aid.

Do we actually believe that every individual who has reported a UFO isn't in control of their faculties? And what part of us chooses to ignore the absolute similarity of these sightings, the way that these objects look and the way they move through the atmosphere?

It is a timely reminder to add that the internet or anything like it was not publicly available in 1978, and it is also indeed a fantastic proposition that people statewide, countrywide and worldwide have somehow all conspired to deceive in a similar way when reporting UFO activity.

My reason for telling this story is to add clarity to the circumstances in which a young person went missing after encountering a UFO over Bass Strait and to vindicate him in his assertion when he said, "It seems to me that he's playing some sort of game. He's flying over me two three times at a time, at speeds I could not identify." And in his effort to identify the craft, stating that "as it's flying past it's a long shape, cannot identify more than that *it has such speed*", logically asking Melbourne if there were any Air Force or military aircraft in the vicinity.

Common characteristics of these craft are that they move at such a speed that is hard to follow by eye but then often stop instantly to hover silently in mid-air.

Does anyone actually believe that Fred could have been covertly studying those flight characteristics with the intention of staging his own disappearance, or even his own grand demise?

This would all assume that he had access to certain descriptive characteristics on previous UFO encounters, information that had been so vigorously denied to the media and the general population of the day.

But also, that his engine was running rough and that his radio communications had failed and the other unmistakable similarities and behavioural characteristics with which the UFO had manoeuvred in the evening sky around him. The speed, the shape, the lights and the colour, being so very typical of other UFO encounters worldwide, which in that pre-internet era, he would've most probably known nothing about.

Or that Vivienne Baldock had also pre-educated herself as to the very distinct behavioural characteristics of UFO sightings worldwide?

As a whole generation has sleepwalked en masse into the everyday post-war patriarchal comfortability of "not rocking the boat" by never questioning authority, this investigation has turned into so much more than that of a missing person.

It has revealed a population that chose to neither ask logical questions nor demand logical answers from their regulators and law enforcement agencies, of their use of tactful deception, and of failing to act appropriately in the execution of their duties.

In this case, failure to act can also be interpreted as lying by omission.

Current-day aviation auditors, when in attendance at small air charter establishments, often resorted to citing administrative errors and typos in the absence of finding anything constituting a genuine threat to air safety, which, once in the hands of a willing bureaucracy, then took months to "clear" in protracted email responses from the air charter operator.

The needless stress generated in these exchanges resulted in many sleepless nights and a dangerous distraction in the workplace born out of frustration and fatigue, which ironically was a threat to the very same air safety that those auditors had been tasked to protect.

In an employer–employee relationship, HR has a name for this, but regrettably, protection only extends to an employee, not to an employer.

True to form on these occasions, closure with respect to items of non-compliance, large or small, never occurred. The closure of an email or even a telephone call had never happened, gifting me an energy and heightening my resolve in the pursuit of matters relating to this investigation and that authority.

As the Irish say, "It's an ill wind that doesn't blow someone some good." And for Fred, this time at least, the wind is firmly at his back.

Perhaps some weren't prone to suspicion about the methods our law enforcement agencies and regulators have employed in the everyday of keeping Australia safe, but it is now ever apparent that, on these occasions at least, we have been played.

Older, post-war Australians were especially inclined to blindly trust authority, but as a result of what I have witnessed in this investigation and in the act of writing this short book, it is apparent that public trust has been abused.

We should be prepared to question authority and seek honest answers to the obvious and logical questions that we ask, especially with respect to this case.

As recently as 2018, I had been told in an official email from our own ATSB that the case was closed in 1982 and will not be re-opened, citing the reasons of aging and unreliable evidence which I, at the time, put down to slothful bureaucracy, of simply refusing to rouse itself, refusing to see.

I know now that they have "seen" very well and that they are practised and ready to act at a moment's notice, to both "hide the truth" and to "protect the people" (if it is possible that those two phrases can share the same sentence and have proper meaning).

The Westall Incident in 1966 was a prime example where the policy was to bully each and every one who had witnessed something so incredible, but now, with the advent and the power of social media, the default may be to remain silent, to simply sit it out and wait for witnesses to suffer the effects of natural attrition. Many already have.

There lies the motivation for me not to waste any more time, and to take the time to write down, not just what I know about Fred, but also what I feel is the right thing to do.

It could very well be time to seek a "Trump-esque" exposé regarding information withheld on both Frederick Valentich and the 1966 Westall Incident.

In my foreword, I declared in a state of naivety:

> *My undertaking is to write this book based on the accumulated knowledge and testimonies, gained over a 25-year period while I owned and operated a small air charter business at Apollo Bay on Victoria's rugged south coast. ...*
>
> *With the information that has been gathered over that period, I am committed to conveying the facts and events as clearly and truthfully as I can, while I still can.*

While the spirit of that transcript is simple and pure, the end result for me has turned out to be much, much more.

The fact that Fred was being stalked and pursued is to me, given the quality and the frequency of witness statements regarding various UFO sightings, including primarily his own, confirmed beyond reasonable doubt.

Pursued by what, and for whatever reason, is not known, and maybe will never be known. But just the fact that there was an independent sighting of an aeroplane apparently in distress in that location on that night, and that there was another player reportedly involved, is again relevant.

So, the big question remains as to the motivation of the investigators, as defined by their underachieving and inaction on the matter.

Was it an example of the old patriarchal society at play, limiting the amount of information that gets out into the public arena because they could?

That's the way they did things then. Control for the sake of control. "The old boys' club."

Or is it to do with suppressing knowledge that was of national importance, information that could potentially spread unrest and panic if made public? After all, isn't that what governments are for, to keep us safe, to manage fear.

Or could it be because this is supremely coveted information, being that of another intelligence, another technology, perhaps the kind of information that can yield unlimited clean energy, or even be used to suppress an aggressor?

Now, at the end of this book, the only energy I sense is dark energy.

Not that of Einstein's mysterious dark energy from outer space, nor the darkness of that unforgiving cold dark Cape Otway coastline and current with its recorded history of tragedy and restless souls.

No, I speak of another lurking darkness.

The dark energy of evasiveness, lies, discreditation and cover-up by those in authority who were entrusted to safeguard the welfare of a young aviator, as was their charter; to locate a young airman who had hopes, dreams and expectations, and the belief that there was someone there to have his back should he need it.

It is a dark energy that has breached the trust of what was then, a very trusting, naïve post-war population, and it stinks. Really stinks.

I ask that the whole enquiry into Frederick Valentich be re-opened, beginning with a search for the lost aircraft, that all documents be made available and, if necessary, the case be reconsidered before a magistrate.

That Fred's dignity should be restored, and he, his then-fiancée Rhonda Rushton and his family, living and deceased, receive an apology for the indignation they have so unjustly been subject to.

That the record of his disappearance should be marked clearly with one finding, words to the effect: "Died by misadventure, due to an encounter with an Unidentified Flying Object."

34

Per ardua ad astra

Through adversity to the stars.
RAAF motto

I do not know for certain what actually happened to Fred that fateful and perfect evening. Who could know?

But I do know, however, that brave young Fred had exactly what it takes to be a good pilot. To be a captain.

He had guts, and from all my enquiries and research, he definitely had determination and skill and that, given his life's many upsides, not the least of which was his attractive young fiancée, Rhonda Rushton, he had plenty to live for.

It is my earnest opinion that for him, suicide was never an option.

An absconder he was not. Choosing to vanish as some say he did is a cowardly accusation, and an accusation penned by cowards.

And neither did he die by misadventure or as a result of piloting incompetence as many who can't handle the truth, for whatever reason, would have us believe.

Fred's death came as a result of having an adventurous soul. An urge in himself that wouldn't be quietened, as is common with all adventurers.

That is, if he is dead.

It is perhaps a concept limited by our own perceptions and experience with the human condition.

Who's to say, even now, that he's not realising his true destiny, piloting a magnificent starship across the heavens. Who can say?

At those inconceivable speeds, the intervening decades may be for him but a few days.

As unbelievable as the story began, it could quite conceivably have an unbelievable ending.

I just know one thing: Fred faced down his destiny alone as he departed the mainland and flew out into the night over a dark, unforgiving ocean.

He did it with a steady hand, an iron nerve and an unwavering spirit, without anyone to steady him or to console him.

How do I know? I know because I could hear it in his voice.

I have sat next to enough young pilots in adverse conditions to understand that one crucial thing: the sound of moral fortitude.

About this, I do not speculate.

I believe it to be the truth.

Plain and simple.

About the Author

Turns out the hardest thing to do is to write about myself.

I started learning to fly in East Africa in 1979 after travelling overland from London. I think of it almost every day.

My first ever excursion in a light plane was from Nairobi down to Mt Kilimanjaro with a doctor from up Lake Turkana way. We flew low over the swamps, and buzzed the herds of elephant and zebra in the Amboseli National Park before lunch at the lodge and I thought to myself, *"wow, isnt flying just teriffic"*.

No one cared then. It was sporting.

It was the beauty of that place that inspired me to maintain a connection with bush flying.

It had been said that we all have a book in us.

I have never at all felt the need to write a book so much as the need to tell this story, and so in that way I see myself as more of a story teller, rather than an author.

In any event it has been a necessary thing for me to do and I am relieved now that it is done.

These days I mostly spend my time evading retirement between my hometown Geelong and a small property in Northeast Victoria.

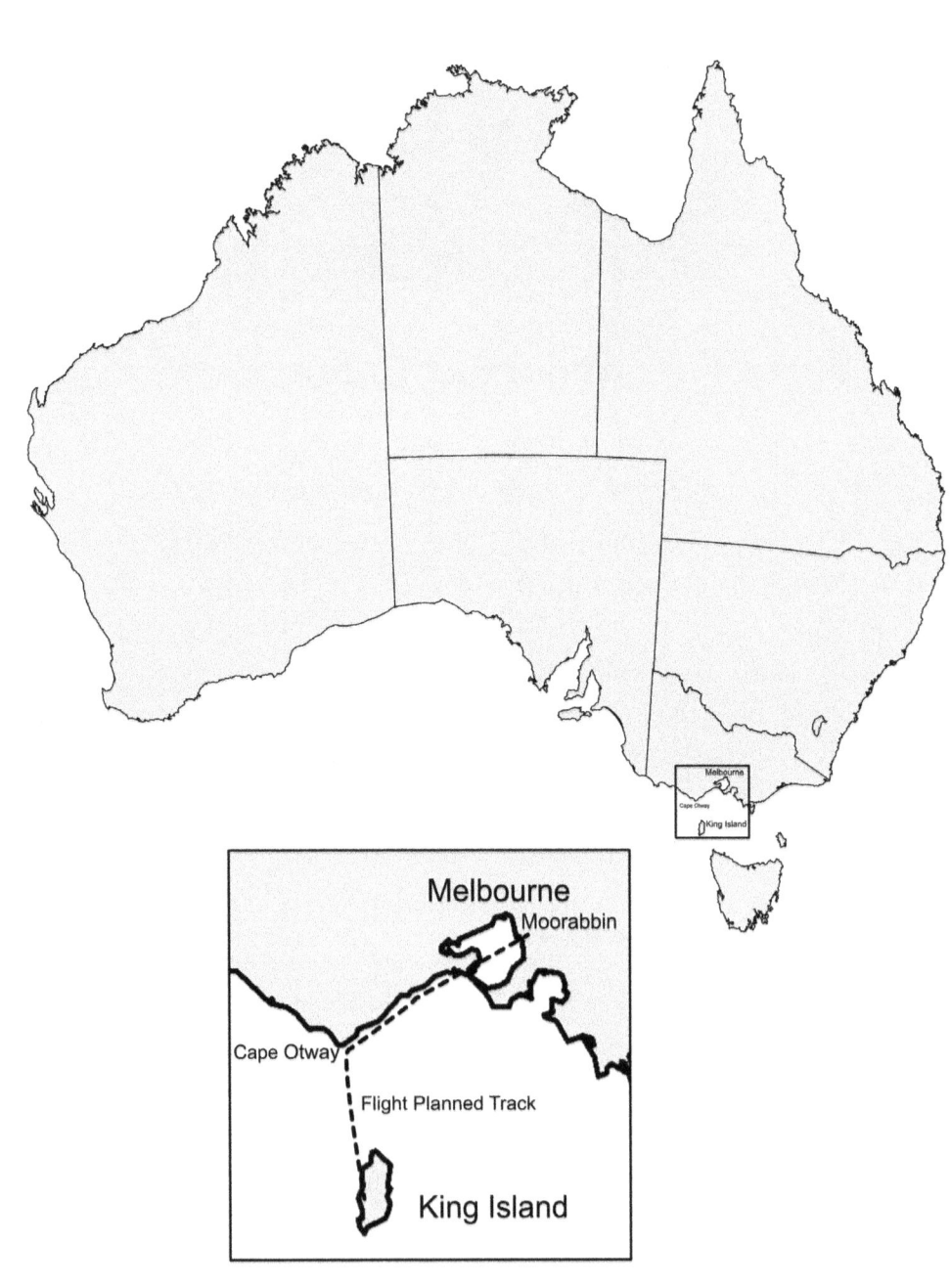

www.ingramcontent.com/pod-product-compliance
Lightning Source LLC
Chambersburg PA
CBHW061218070526
44584CB00029B/3878